PRESENTED TO:

_____

PRESENTED BY:

_____

DATE

_____

Rest in Hope: 90 Devotions of God's Comfort and Care
© 2018 DaySpring Cards, Inc. All rights reserved.
First Edition, January 2019

Published by:
P.O. Box 1010
Siloam Springs, AR 72761
dayspring.com

Written by Jennifer Gerelds
Designed by Greg Jackson of thinkpen.design

Printed in China
Prime: 89888
ISBN: 9781684086160

REST IN HOPE

90
DEVOTIONS
OF GOD'S
COMFORT
AND CARE

JENNIFER GERELDS

TABLE OF CONTENTS

INTRODUCTION:
TIME FOR REST

It's hard for most of us to put a finger on it, really. *What is it* that makes us try so hard at (or in some cases avoid) the life we find set before us? As if on autopilot, we wake up each morning driven by the day's agenda, propelling us out of our beds and into action. We have work to accomplish. Schedules to keep. Church activities to attend. People to experience (and strive to please). *Life to live.* We're never certain what we will encounter in our unrelenting race, but we know one thing's for sure: unless something monumental stops us, we have to keep going. Keep pushing. Keep striving. If we don't, won't we miss out? Or worse, *won't things fall apart?* we subconsciously worry.

But what if our worst fears are *unfounded*, a cultural misconception that keeps us from truth? What if our pursuits are precisely the reason we're reeling from exhaustion and unable to experience the peace and security we crave? What if the best way to win at life's race is to rest instead of run harder?

Jesus says it is.

Time after time throughout all of Scripture, God invites, calls, and even commands His people to rest from their efforts to be God...to be still and remember something important, a reality we can't see when our minds and lives are filled with the clamor of constant activity: God alone is in charge and has a plan bigger and better than ours. He, the Sovereign One, is God...and we are not.

When we remember this fundamental truth, two miracles unfold. First, we find delightful freedom. It is amazing how light our hearts feel when we know that someone stronger and more capable than us shoulders our burdens. Then, as we witness His faithfulness and sufficiency in our struggles, we find our souls able to settle into true trust. Surrender to and trust in our more-than-capable and loving Father ushers us into lasting peace and promised rest.

Could you use a little R & R in your life right now—and always? *Rest in Hope* is a ninety-day devotional sabbatical from the pull-yourself-up-by-the-bootstraps burden found everywhere else today. It invites you daily into the greater reality of God's goodness and provision already made for you. In His presence alone, your soul will find the perspective, hope, and peace you need for this day.

THE DIVINE DECREE

By the seventh day God had finished
His work, and so He rested.

GENESIS 2:2 CEV

Every time you round that corner in your house, you see him curled up in a ball on his favorite chair—the one that once served people but now has become a rather royal bed for your beloved cat. "Must be nice," you mutter, as you give him a quick stroke behind the ears. "How do you sleep all day?" For just a quick second, you ponder what it's like to be a cat. How would it feel to rest like that and not feel bad about it?

It isn't just our pets that give us a picture of rest. Every other kind of living creature does, too. Yet as humans, we feel exempt from this part of the created order. For sure, work is necessary—a God-ordained command and calling. But we have to wonder about our balance when we doze at traffic lights and yawn throughout our meetings. Our bodies are sending a signal that our kindhearted Creator wants us to hear: we all need rest, from the tips of our toes to the depths of our souls.

The great news is that we can choose rest without guilt. Better still, God says we must rest—not only physically but also spiritually—if we want to really know Him. His divine permission unfolds in the first few pages of Scripture when He rested from His important work, and His call to follow suit fills the rest of His written Word. Only when we stop striving can we recharge our bodies and refocus our minds to the truth of who we are: humans fully dependent on God and designed to follow His lead in every way.

························

THEN HE SAID TO THEM,
"THE SABBATH WAS MADE FOR MAN,
NOT MAN FOR THE SABBATH."

MARK 2:27 NIV

GREEN PASTURES IN THE PRESENT

The LORD is my shepherd, I lack nothing.
He makes me lie down in green pastures,
He leads me beside quiet waters,
He refreshes my soul.

PSALM 23:1–3 NIV

That familiar feeling of panic is about to set in, and you feel it rising from the pit of your stomach straight to your head. As if on steroids, your mind races ahead of the emotion, rehearsing all the details that must be done or fall into place before you can finally get a grip. In the moment (and it turns out there are many of these moments every day), it feels like so much is at stake if you fail. Fear grips you and threatens to sabotage your plans, your work—and ultimately your worth.

But as always, fear is a liar. If you are God's child, you are not on your own, struggling to pull all the necessary strings to make life work in your favor. With Jesus at your side, you lack nothing! His all-powerful hand leads you through life's twists and turns, always providing access to the calm, gentle streams of His indwelling spirit. No matter how crazy the day gets, God's presence with you in it is a verdant pasture of peace for your soul.

Today, if you feel panicked about an upcoming project or problem, don't let your mind race with all the what-ifs. Instead, put your mind and heart to rest by remembering that your God has this day—and your life—in His hands. Let the Shepherd lead you through each moment as you acknowledge His presence and goodness in it. Look to Him for guidance and lie down in His promised care.

THE LORD MAKES FIRM THE STEPS
OF THE ONE WHO DELIGHTS IN HIM;
THOUGH HE MAY STUMBLE,
HE WILL NOT FALL, FOR THE LORD
UPHOLDS HIM WITH HIS HAND.
I WAS YOUNG AND NOW I AM OLD,
YET I HAVE NEVER SEEN
THE RIGHTEOUS FORSAKEN OR
THEIR CHILDREN BEGGING BREAD.

PSALM 37:23–25 NIV

TUCKED AWAY

They marched for three days after leaving the mountain of the
LORD, with the Ark of the LORD's Covenant moving ahead
of them to show them where to stop and rest. As they moved
on each day, the cloud of the LORD hovered over them.

NUMBERS 10:33–34 NLT

The room smelled of finger paint and playdough, the class of kindergarteners working steadily at their stations, when their teacher made the call: "Time to put up your work and get out your mats," she announced cheerfully. A few kids grumbled, resisting her assistance, but most went without incident to the mats designated for their daily rest. With lights off and mouths closed, the once-rowdy children soon drifted off to sleep, their tiny bodies refueling energy for all that lay ahead.

Like the teacher, people who know children understand the importance of rest for growing, healthy young minds and bodies. In a similar way, God knows what His children need— even when we're convinced we need to keep going. He goes before us, providing pockets of time for needed rest tucked into each day when we can turn our minds and cares over to Him. But unlike the teacher, He doesn't force the issue. We must be willing to be still when the moment presents itself. Instead of turning on the radio, surfing the Web, or scrolling through social media whenever there's a lull, let your attention turn to God and His Word. Allow yourself time to rest in stillness, simply thinking about who He is and how He cares for you. At the end of the day, you will find that your time was never wasted. Instead, your mind and soul's rest today readies you for all God has in store for you tomorrow.

••••••••••••••••••••••

YOUR FATHER KNOWS WHAT YOU
NEED BEFORE YOU ASK HIM.

MATTHEW 6:8 NIV

STORM SHELTER

Whoever dwells in the shelter
of the Most High will rest
in the shadow of the Almighty.

PSALM 91:1 NIV

You can remember the moments like they were just yesterday—those chilling childhood memories when the terror of a night's dream or a clapping crash of a thunderstorm outside your window woke and worried you. Crouching low under the covers simply wouldn't cut it. Fear moved you out of your bedroom in search of a safer, more substantial place of shelter. Slipping silently between your parents even as they slept, your pounding heart quieted. Your panic stilled as your breathing fell in sync with theirs. Nestled next to them, you felt safe, surrounded by such powerful love.

As you grew up, though, so did your knowledge of the world. You learned: earthly parents—and people in general—aren't fail-proof. Real-life problems don't always disappear with the dawn. Fearful unknowns like insufficient finances, broken relationships, and failing health can leave you feeling like you did as a child, powerless to calm the mounting pressures all around you. Only this time, our problems are greater than any parent can solve...except our heavenly Father.

Child of God, you don't need to stay stuck in your fears, afraid of what is to come, wondering who can help. Leave the isolation of self-reliance and turn to God Almighty. He is a shield and source of comfort like no other. Not only is He right beside us, He is above us, below us, before us, and behind us! Better still, He put His Spirit *in* us so we can sleep, wake, and walk in total confidence that we remain always in His competent and constant care.

....

BUT AS FOR ME,
IT IS GOOD TO BE NEAR GOD.
I HAVE MADE THE
SOVEREIGN LORD MY REFUGE.

PSALM 73:28 NIV

BE CARRIED

*Then Jesus said, "Come to Me, all of you who are weary
and carry heavy burdens, and I will give you rest. Take My
yoke upon you. Let Me teach you, because I am humble
and gentle at heart, and you will find rest for your souls.*

MATTHEW 11:28–29 NLT

It was supposed to be fun, according to the brochure. All you
had to do to be certified to scuba dive was to complete a short
training session, one that required you to swim the length of the
pool and back a few times to demonstrate your ability. *No problem*, you think—until you step up to the pool's edge. "We have
to put a weight belt around you to simulate diving conditions,"
they announce. A million arguments mount in your mind
against the idea but they fasten the belt anyway, and you begin
the now extremely difficult feat of swimming with all the extra
weight. Before you've crossed the pool even once, exhaustion
sets in and you start to think, *Maybe scuba diving isn't for me!*

Unfortunately, many people come to the same conclusion
about their spiritual lives. They hear that a relationship with God
is supposed to bring peace and joy, but they find that some of
the religious leaders and even thoughts in their own mind are

weighing them down with performance requirements too heavy to carry. *Being a Christian is just another burden,* they conclude.

But the truth brings blessed relief! Jesus beckons us to take on His yoke—His way of living—instead of the impossible burdens we find ourselves carrying on our own. Instead of weighing us down, His belt of truth actually buoys our spirits, filling our hearts with light, hope, and all the power we need to finish all the good works He has planned for us to do. Following Jesus His way frees us from all guilt and condemnation, fuels our hearts with unending love, and propels us toward our life purpose. And nothing's more fun than that!

• • • • • • • • • • • • • • • • • • • •

BUT WHATEVER WERE GAINS TO ME I NOW CONSIDER
LOSS FOR THE SAKE OF CHRIST. WHAT IS MORE,
I CONSIDER EVERYTHING A LOSS BECAUSE OF THE
SURPASSING WORTH OF KNOWING CHRIST JESUS MY
LORD, FOR WHOSE SAKE I HAVE LOST ALL THINGS. I
CONSIDER THEM GARBAGE, THAT I MAY GAIN CHRIST
AND BE FOUND IN HIM, NOT HAVING A RIGHTEOUSNESS
OF MY OWN THAT COMES FROM THE LAW, BUT THAT
WHICH IS THROUGH FAITH IN CHRIST—THE RIGHTEOUSNESS
THAT COMES FROM GOD ON THE BASIS OF FAITH.

PHILIPPIANS 3:7–9 NIV

PRICELESS REST

Is anyone thirsty?
Come and drink—
even if you have no money!
Come, take your choice
of wine or milk—
it's all free!

ISAIAH 55:1 NLT

Last month it was your turn. Your daughter got married and you pulled out all the stops to make it a wonderful memory. But the detailed planning and provision for the large event took quite a toll on your savings. *So much for retiring early*, you thought.

But today is different. You've been invited to someone else's party, and you don't have to prepare a thing. Upon arrival, you notice tables filled to overflowing with every kind of treat imaginable, with drinks all free for the taking as well. It doesn't take long for you to settle in, surround yourself with friends, and splurge on all the free goodness provided for you!

So guess what it's going to be like in heaven? The God of all creation has prepared a wedding feast for His people like no other party on our planet. Everything we could wish for and then some will be provided at no cost to us—at all!

But God's celebration over His people doesn't start at some future time. It begins the very moment we decide to accept His invitation to come to Him. At no cost to us, God provides a feast of divine riches that are all ours for the taking because of our connection to Jesus. Are you out of wisdom? He's got that. Could you use a little joy? There's a fountain of it right here. Are you craving real and lasting relationship? You've come right to the place. The one thing He asks is that we leave our baggage with Him at the door. He knows just where to dispose of it. He's even got your party clothes covered, courtesy of Jesus, who already paid for it all.

THEY FEAST ON THE ABUNDANCE OF YOUR HOUSE; YOU GIVE THEM DRINK FROM YOUR RIVER OF DELIGHTS.

PSALM 36:8 NIV

FEAST OF KINGS

You prepare a feast for me
in the presence of my enemies.
You honor me by anointing my head with oil.
My cup overflows with blessings.
Surely your goodness and unfailing love will pursue me
all the days of my life,
and I will live in the house of the LORD
forever.

PSALM 23:5–6 NLT

At this moment, for different reasons, all your important relationships seem on the rocks. Your mother is frustrated with your infrequent visits. Your neighbors complain about how you keep your yard. Your kids get mouthy when you make them put away their phones, and your spouse said something sarcastic that sent your mind spinning with anger and worry. *They are not my enemies!* you mentally remind yourself as you try to keep your composure through all the relational interactions. But sometimes it feels as if they really are your enemies, leaving you feeling isolated and alone, your heart in utter unrest.

So picture this: All the people in your life who put different demands on you are standing in a circle around you. But in the center of it all, you're seated at a table overflowing with incredible food. Beside you sits Jesus, the King of all creation. He has prepared this feast before you and offers an exclusive opportunity for you to dine with Him—in perfect peace. Would you put everything else aside and focus on His favor, or would you continue to fret about everyone else around you?

Where we place our focus determines our level of peace in the present moment. Psalm 23 tells us that God does, in fact, prepare tables of delight right in front of our enemies, and He invites us to come and sit in the comfort of His company—no matter what mayhem swirls around you.

Today, will you turn your attention from all that seems wrong to see the Savior who faithfully stays by your side, supplying an abundance of goodness in the fellowship?

* * * * * * * * * * * * * * * * * * * *

LOOK! I HAVE BEEN STANDING AT THE DOOR, AND I AM CONSTANTLY KNOCKING. IF ANYONE HEARS ME CALLING HIM AND OPENS THE DOOR, I WILL COME IN AND FELLOWSHIP WITH HIM AND HE WITH ME.

REVELATION 3:20 TLB

PERFECT POSTURE

We have freedom now because Christ made us free. So stand
strong. Do not change and go back into the slavery of the law.

GALATIANS 5:1 ICB

I't's not that we don't know better. Oodles of times we've heard
our parents, teachers, and physicians tell us, "You need to sit
up straight." Posture is important! When we slump, our mus-
cles fatigue and back pain inevitably ensues. And yet a curious phenomenon occurs as we drive long hours or sit at the
computer. Slowly our shoulders start to sink, sometimes until
they're almost in our laps! Gravity seems to take its toll despite
our best intentions.

Spiritually speaking, God's people fight another similar di-
lemma even more damaging than poor posture: we slip out of
alignment with the truth of God's grace. Though we know our
salvation was a gift, we slowly start sinking back into a performance posture with God, trying to earn and keep His favor
by our record. But like our parents and teachers, the apostle
Paul warns us: *Watch your posture!* Don't let your minds slip
back into a performance mentality. Jesus already finished the
work of flawless living—followed by sacrificing His own life—

that won God's favor on your behalf. You are now free to rest in God's unchanging affection, reaching your full potential through the power of Christ inside you.

Have you felt your spiritual posture slipping lately, sinking back into the wrong belief that God only loves you when you get it right? Our secure position in Christ and God's favor rests on God's incredible provision, not our performance. Confess the sin of self-reliance and sit up straight under the truth of God's grace, head held high with confidence as a chosen and beloved child of the King!

••••••••••••••••••••••

WE WHO HAVE BELIEVED ARE ABLE TO ENTER AND HAVE GOD'S REST.

HEBREWS 4:3 ICB

THE PEACE PARADOX

You, Lord, give true peace.
You give peace to those who depend on You.
You give peace to those who trust You....
Lord, all our success is because of what You have done.
So give us peace.

ISAIAH 26:3, 12 ICB

Before you even head out the door, you know by experience what's about to unfold. Months ago you agreed to volunteer at your church's VBS (thank the Lord you're not the one in charge). You simply agreed to show up and carry out whatever need they had...which turned out to be a class leader. Before you started to stress, though, the coordinator handed you the schedule, the script, and everything you needed to sail smoothly through the day. Though far from flawless, you still watched all the pieces fall into place with a small crowd of children knowing Jesus better in the end, a paradoxically exhausting and exhilarating experience.

Such is the mysterious nature of God, who calls us to work and rest in the same breath. Work to believe. Rest because faith is a gift. Work out your salvation. Rest because God is the One really doing all the work in you. There is peace when we work in obedience, resting in God's provision—the paradox of true Christian living.

When Jesus invites His people to rest in His hope and peace, He isn't promising an easy or pain-free life. To the contrary, He guarantees that we will encounter trouble, a by-product of our broken, sinful world. The incredible news is that He has overcome the world and our problems in it. Like the VBS experience, He has already written the script and orchestrated every moment of history for His glory and the good of His people. Our part? We show up. We make ourselves available to do what only He can, what He chooses to do through us. We actively participate in God's work while our souls stay at rest, knowing He's in charge and has planned it all according to His purpose.

••••••••••••••••••••••

JESUS ANSWERED,
"THE WORK OF GOD IS THIS:
TO BELIEVE IN THE ONE
HE HAS SENT."

JOHN 6:29 NIV

27

INVITED TO COME

The Spirit and the bride say, "Come."
Let anyone who hears this say, "Come."
REVELATION 22:17 NLT

Your spouse is turning fifty. Already he has mentioned, on more than one occasion, how much he'd like to reconnect with all his friends. So you begin to plan a party, one that will celebrate a life of special relationships. As you pull out all the stops, planning food, decorations, and places for everyone to sit, you ponder who to include. Invitations go out, and the waiting begins. After awhile a few RSVPs come back, but you can't help but feel a little nervous. What if no one comes? What if everyone you ask is already busy with work and kids and the other million calendar fillers that keep us all so disconnected?

What if that's a little taste of how God feels about us?

After all, He has planned not just a party, but an entirely new life for every person who comes into His kingdom. He invites us to come and take part in the extravagance of His provision and love, connecting with other people who have chosen to come. But an invitation remains only that, if we don't respond. If we carry on with our worrisome ways, packing in even more activities in our hectic schedules, striving so hard for some semblance of the good life, but miss the spectacular opportunity that lies before us—what will we reap? Fleeting moments of happiness are a sad substitute for the life of eternal blessing and hope God has planned to last forever.

Today, don't turn down God's invitation to rest in His sovereign goodness. Turn from the temptation to plot your own life's course and pursue, instead, God's path to perfect peace through relationship with Jesus. Let the party begin!

THEN HE SENT SOME MORE SERVANTS AND SAID, "TELL THOSE WHO HAVE BEEN INVITED THAT I HAVE PREPARED MY DINNER: MY OXEN AND FATTENED CATTLE HAVE BEEN BUTCHERED, AND EVERYTHING IS READY. COME TO THE WEDDING BANQUET."

MATTHEW 22:4 NIV

REMEMBER WHO GOD IS

Do you not know? Have you not heard?...
Your Maker is your husband—
the Lord Almighty is His name—
the Holy One of Israel is your Redeemer;
He is called the God of all the earth.

ISAIAH 40:28, 54:5 NIV

You're starting to wonder if your entire family has a hearing problem. You feel certain you've asked the kids at least three times to clean up their mess, though it lingers still on the kitchen counter. And last time you checked, the very simple to-do list you left with your spouse is only halfway finished. It's hard, really hard, not to blow a gasket. But even under the simmering anger there's a more sinister fear lurking, though you work diligently to keep it suppressed. *Your control methods aren't working.* In fact, you can't get anyone to do anything that you want—that you desperately feel like you need. And if you're honest, at times you feel utterly helpless. Is there anyone reliable out there to come to your rescue?

Fortunately, the answer is yes! But you won't find your hero in your family or even your friends. The truth is, we don't just need clean counters and competent spouses to have peaceful hearts. We all need *saving*—including the people we secretly hope will make all of our anxieties and problems go away. Only one person on our planet, and in the entire universe, possesses the power to deliver us out of our current predicament, as well as position us for our eternal home in heaven, and it's Jesus. The One who created us calls Himself our Husband, sworn to uphold, protect, and provide for His people for as long as we both shall live...which is forever with Him. When we recognize that God is the very present help we need, we can rest assured that He will give us the grace, patience, and love we need to handle life's challenges well.

. . . .

THE LORD IS THE EVERLASTING GOD,
THE CREATOR OF THE ENDS OF THE EARTH.
HE WILL NOT GROW TIRED OR WEARY,
AND HIS UNDERSTANDING NO ONE CAN FATHOM.

ISAIAH 40:28 NIV

FAMILY BLESSING

*Since you are God's children, God sent the Spirit of His
Son into your hearts, and the Spirit cries out, "Father."*

GALATIANS 4:6 NCV

It felt so foreign, this new life of love that she, a former orphan, was now feeling. Meetings had happened, papers were signed, transactions had finished. And now this young child was surrounded by new family and friends who loved her as if she had been there all along! Though she had not learned their language, their hearts spoke clearly through the hugs and smiles that encircled her. Her former life had been filled with pain. Now, she was finally home.

So it is with every person who places their trust in Jesus. When we enter into relationship with God, we step into a family bound by a love beyond our wildest dreams. Before time even began, before the first star began to shine, our triune God lived out the love that is His very nature. Father, Son, and Holy Spirit served One another in perfect unity, adding angels as witnesses to the wonderful bond. But as love always does, it expands. It grows. And God created people to share in the bliss of His perfect, beautiful, boundless love.

Today, let the love of God's forever family free you from your fears of abandonment. You will never walk another step without God right beside you, His Son covering you, and His Spirit filling you with the fruit of His incredible presence. You are a part of God's family blessing, and by our Father's grace you will bring that blessing to all you encounter this day.

* * *

SO GO AND MAKE FOLLOWERS
OF ALL PEOPLE IN THE WORLD.
BAPTIZE THEM IN THE NAME
OF THE FATHER AND THE SON
AND THE HOLY SPIRIT.

MATTHEW 28:19 NCV

HUNGRY SOULS

He proved He is real by showing kindness, by giving
you rain from heaven and crops at the right times, by
giving you food and filling your hearts with joy.
ACTS 14:17 NCV

If you could bottle the moment, it would sell for over a million dollars. Actually, it's priceless—this peace you feel—as your family sits gathered around the table, laughing and sharing the day's stories. Your soul stirs. *Something deep is happening here*, you realize, though you're not sure of the source. You simply know, *This is good. We were made for this.* And your heart overflows with thanks.

More than the food, we crave belonging. We crave connections that confirm we are not alone—and never will be. We long for confidence that the good will not only last but grow stronger as time goes on. It's an appetite for eternal love and community, the kind our hungry souls seek to have satisfied.

For many the search persists, with only momentary pleasures patching the deeper ache. What on earth are we to do with this raging need no place or person on earth can permanently ease?

The Father says to come. Sit at the table of eternal provision He offers through relationship with His Son. Breathe in His reality through His written Word, and rest from your wearying quest to satisfy the search elsewhere. With unlimited resources and riches, our Father stands ready to supply all that you need.

What worries you today? Are you afraid you can't make ends meet? That your future plans will fail? That you'll lose someone you love? Child of God, your Father knows...and He will fully satisfy the deepest needs of your body and soul.

······················

SO ABRAHAM NAMED THAT PLACE THE LORD
PROVIDES. EVEN TODAY PEOPLE SAY, "ON THE
MOUNTAIN OF THE LORD IT WILL BE PROVIDED."
GENESIS 22:14 NCV

COVERED IN CONFIDENCE

My shield is God Most High,
who saves the upright in heart.
PSALM 7:10 NIV

When you were a kid, you didn't think twice about going outside to play. Blue summer skies beckoned you to build forts, ride bikes, and simply explore the outside world. You experienced endless hours of pure, unadulterated, worry-free fun in the sun—until scientists discovered the secret harm in some of the sun's rays. Diligent parents all over the planet began coating themselves and their kids in sunscreen so they could continue enjoying the sun's warmth without the skin cancer–causing side effects.

In a way, our souls experience a similar shift spiritually as we transition from the blissful innocence of childhood to the harsh realities of adult life. Painful past experiences magnify the potential for future disappointments, leaving you paralyzed with fear in the present. It can make you want to stay inside your own walled-up world so you don't have to risk getting hurt "out there." But when we withdraw, we don't really live.

So what is a fearful Christian supposed to do? You guessed it. Apply Son screen! It might sound silly—even childish—at first. But when you take the time to apply the truth of your redemption by Christ's blood, you can embrace life completely confident that you are covered in God's eternal favor. No accusation, condemnation, shame, guilt, or pain can ever harm who you are as a child of God. God's grace—His permanent presence in our lives—is our shield who empowers us to take the risk of really living by loving well. We were made to enjoy God and His world with childlike abandon, trusting Him to protect and lead us through life's every adventure.

AFTER THIS, THE WORD OF THE LORD
CAME TO ABRAM IN A VISION:
"DO NOT BE AFRAID, ABRAM.
I AM YOUR SHIELD,
YOUR VERY GREAT REWARD."

GENESIS 15:1 NIV

RISING UP

Guide me in Your truth and teach me,
for You are God my Savior,
and my hope is in You all day long.

PSALM 25:5 NIV

You didn't know it was coming. Maybe you heard warnings, but you didn't believe the forecasters when they showed the telltale mass of white clouds swirling like a pinwheel on their radars. You'd weathered hurricanes before. Why would this one be any different?

But then the floodwaters rose—not inch by inch, but foot by foot. You watched your home sink beneath its surge, you and your family climbing higher and higher trying to save yourselves. But the roof is all that's left, and you feel your home's foundation sway. You're in more trouble than you ever imagined. And you've never understood more intensely your need for saving.

Sometimes it takes desperate situations for our deepest needs to reach the surface of our understanding. Maybe we find ourselves caught up in a habit that's destroying our family. Maybe we've made a wreck of the relationships around us. Or maybe just the emptiness in our hearts starts aching too much to ignore and the realization dawns: we're in more trouble than we ever imagined...and nothing on earth can save us now.

But we have a God in heaven who will. It's in His name and it's who He is, Savior of the world. Whether we seek power for the present problem or eternal salvation for our souls, Jesus delivers what no one else on earth can: assurance. When we rest in Him, our rescue is guaranteed. In our utter weakness, we watch in awe and wonder at God's saving grace.

* *

OUR GOD IS A GOD WHO SAVES;
FROM THE SOVEREIGN LORD COMES
ESCAPE FROM DEATH.

PSALM 68:20 NIV

RELIABILITY RATING

*Praise the LORD who has given rest to His people Israel,
just as He promised. Not one word has failed of all the
wonderful promises He gave through His servant Moses.*

I KINGS 8:56 NLT

It's not my fault, you reason, explaining the uneasiness that urges you to keep checking up on everyone else's progress. Yes, you know your spouse is a capable and intelligent person. But you've learned from past experience that reliability wouldn't truthfully top his résumé. And your coworkers are no problem when they keep to their own projects. But joint ventures are just so stressful. You never know if others will actually pull through on their end, and you don't want to be left picking up the pieces. Micromanagement seems to be the only realistic option. It may make you—and others—miserable, but you want and feel like you need concrete resolution more.

But God offers another solution. You *do* have one Friend who is flawlessly faithful—not only to come through for you in a pinch but to provide the stability your uncertain soul craves. The Bible says God's faithfulness reaches to the heavens! Why not take a moment and look up at the sky to see how far that is?

Do you believe Him? God's ways are not like ours, and neither are His thoughts. He doesn't shift like shadows or turn His back when the going gets tough. Our God is faithful now and forever, His reliability rating higher than the universe itself.

Rest comes when we realize that our hope lies in our God, who literally cannot fail us. It would go against His very nature. So we *can* relax—even when others fall short. We have a God who always has our back.

. . . .

THE LORD PASSED IN FRONT
OF MOSES, CALLING OUT,
"YAHWEH! THE LORD!
THE GOD OF COMPASSION AND MERCY!
I AM SLOW TO ANGER
AND FILLED WITH UNFAILING LOVE
AND FAITHFULNESS."

EXODUS 34:6 NLT

THE GAME CHANGER

The LORD gave them rest on every side, just as He had
sworn to their ancestors. Not one of their enemies withstood
them; the LORD gave all their enemies into their hands.

JOSHUA 21:44 NIV

You know it's just Little League. On the scale of eternity, this one soccer game doesn't even matter. But the other team is cutthroat, the little dribblers taking cheap shots at your child's teammates. When one of the biggest bullies shoves your child to the dirt, you're up from your seat in a millisecond screaming "Foul!" to the ref.

It may be just a game, but still it stirs something powerful deep within. *We want good to win.* It's why we grip our seats through thrilling movies where our hero fights against foe after foe—and we fear that all is lost. Yet in some twist of fate, he finds that one narrow path to victory and we can breathe again. As the credits roll, our souls rest for a brief moment and revel in the glory we feel is somehow our own.

And that's because it is. God won it for us through His only Son's sacrificial death and hell-defeating resurrection. As followers of Jesus, we will see the battle between good and evil unfolding on every front—from outside threats and lies to the sinister sin inside our own hearts. It may even, at times, feel like we've lost the fight and we're tempted to give up. But believer, take heart. Your God has overcome the world. Press on and fight the good fight, and you will, too. You're on the winning team!

FOR YOU, LORD, HAVE
DELIVERED ME FROM DEATH,
MY EYES FROM TEARS,
MY FEET FROM STUMBLING,
THAT I MAY WALK BEFORE THE LORD
IN THE LAND OF THE LIVING.

PSALM 116:8–9 NIV

CONSTANT COMPANION

For a minute, you contemplate just chucking your phone out the car window. Thanks to technology, you no longer enjoy the natural boundary created by leaving the workplace. Now it follows you everywhere you go, along with the almost endless demands of not only bosses but other people you aim to please. You're not a negative person, but you are a perceptive one. And you're afraid if you fold or fail in any arena, you just might forfeit that relationship. People's loyalties just don't seem to last as long these days.

But then you arrive home, greeted by your ever-faithful furry friend. Excited circles, barks, and then almost manic kisses calm your fretful mind. You sit on the foyer floor, and instantly your dog rolls over, exposing his belly for better petting. To him, you can do no wrong. And as you let the day's worries melt away in his soft fur, your soul recalls the Source of such goodness.

God gives us glimpses of His heart through the comfort His creatures provide. Like your faithful companion, only infinitely better, God's affection for you never wavers. No matter how successful you are or how badly you fail, your heavenly Father never leaves your side. He never walks away, because our God is loyal like no other. Every confession is met with forgiveness, every concern resolved with compassion. Don't let the world's demands bring you down. Rest instead in the comfort of God's constant friendship, the God who never lets you go.

RETURN TO YOUR REST,
MY SOUL, FOR THE LORD
HAS BEEN GOOD TO YOU.

PSALM 116:7 NIV

FASHIONED
FOR ETERNITY

He has made everything beautiful in its time.
He has also set eternity in the human heart;
yet no one can fathom what God has
done from beginning to end.

ECCLESIASTES 3:11 NIV

The eighties are back. Just a simple stroll past each store-front window in your nearest shopping plaza will display the trend. High-waisted shorts with crop tops suit the mannequins just fine, but for someone who actually remembers when that fashion idea first started? Well, maybe those bell bottoms would be a better choice.

It's funny how adding a little age to your perspective alters what you perceive as important. What seemed so critical to you as a young kid (like winning that game or getting that toy) now ranks at utterly irrelevant compared to today's concerns. Much like fashion trends, what we worry about changes with our life's seasons. Hindsight tells us that much of the minutiae that drained our mental and physical energy didn't matter all that much in the end.

But we weren't made for insignificance. Believers in Jesus belong to a God who is eternal, and He has put that longing into our hearts. The frivolous life isn't for us anymore. God leads us through our longing to live for what lasts forever. When we walk in our destiny to receive and give God's love, we live every moment for His glory into eternity.

When you feel the floodwaters of stress rising around you, remember to add God's age to your perspective. The God who was and is and is to come is with you right now in this present moment. If you will surrender your plans and desires to His purpose and direction, your path, moment by moment, will take on eternal importance. Rest and realize that in God's hands, our ordinary lives wield extraordinary impact.

• •

TRUST IN THE LORD FOREVER,
FOR THE LORD, THE LORD HIMSELF,
IS THE ROCK ETERNAL.

ISAIAH 26:4 NIV

SHEPHERD

God, my shepherd!
I don't need a thing.
You have bedded me down in lush meadows,
You find me quiet pools to drink from.
True to Your word,
You let me catch my breath
and send me in the right direction.
PSALM 23:1–3 THE MESSAGE

It is early morning, and you secretly slip away from your sleeping spouse and children for some alone time on the dock. In the break of dawn, the warm sunrays reflect a sparkling gold on still, green water, inviting you down the well-worn path to the languid lake below. No boats or Jet Skis make a sound. Only the gentle wind rustles its way through leafy trees, the birds not yet awake from their slumber. Reaching the landing, you plop onto the waiting chair and breathe in deeply the earthy air.

Why do calm waters settle our soul? What is it in the sensation of stillness that sets our minds at ease?

Maybe in those moments we taste our rightful place in God's created order. Surrounded by the simple beauty of what He has made, our souls drink in the truth of who He is. God is our Shepherd who leads us to still waters and restores our souls. In the stillness, we remember His grandeur. In the quiet, we hear His Spirit whisper words of refreshing life, the precious promise of His protective, paternal presence. We bask in His love.

But the sun rises higher, the day's activities ready to unfold. You also rise from your rest, though your soul stays seated in the comfort of your Shepherd's care. Your heart and mind are fixed on following His lead every step in this day, trusting His kindness to take you where you need to go, guiding you all the way.

•••••••••••••••••••••••

I AM THE GOOD SHEPHERD.
THE GOOD SHEPHERD LAYS DOWN
HIS LIFE FOR THE SHEEP.

JOHN 10:11 NIV

BLAZE OF GLORY

There is no one holy like the LORD;
there is no one besides You;
there is no Rock like our God.

1 SAMUEL 2:2 NIV

He was alone in the desert when he first encountered God's all-consuming fire. The blaze that burned no branch or leaf mesmerized Moses for a moment before the fearful reality dawned: *Who sees God's face and lives?* Surely he was doomed. And yet, by some strange mercy, Moses still stood, though his sandals were now removed in reverence. Here, by the Fire, his life-purpose unfolded. "Set My people free!" God said.

And so the story unfolds, God's purposed salvation provided through a humble shepherd who obeyed because he saw God's glory. Later, the delivered people saw it too, when they gathered near Mt. Sinai to hear and learn the ways of God's holiness. To walk with Him, they must walk like Him—perfect to the core. Standing at a distance, the people watched the mountain quake, the fiery billows burn and churn around the mountain's peak. Creation crashed and flashed in awe of its Creator's presence.

"It's too much for us!" they cried. They needed someone to stand between them and their God.

And we do, too. Even today, God's holy fire hasn't dimmed, despite the darkness of our world. To walk with a holy God we must be holy like Him—a fearful task, knowing our daily failures. Like the Israelites, we all need someone to stand between us and the flames. So God Himself forged a way.

Jesus became our holiness. Hidden in Him, we are invited to approach the mountain of God's holy presence, in fearful reverence but with hearts at rest. God welcomes us to fellowship with Him face-to-face through Jesus. Then, like Moses, we heed His call to go and set sin's captives free.

* *

SPEAK TO THE ENTIRE ASSEMBLY OF ISRAEL
AND SAY TO THEM: "BE HOLY BECAUSE
I, THE LORD YOUR GOD, AM HOLY."

LEVITICUS 19:2 NIV

SOVEREIGN

For You have been my hope, Sovereign LORD,
my confidence since my youth.

PSALM 71:5 NIV

Her parents could barely breathe as they watched, their hearts pounding in their chests as if they were the ones up on that beam. Gracefully, the little girl-turned-teen moved nimbly across the narrow plank as if it were a valley wide. Back flip, front flip, with an occasional dance between breathtaking maneuvers, she kept her rhythm just as she had practiced thousands of times before. Serious, but with no sign of fear, she simply focused her eyes straight ahead at some invisible point on her mind's horizon. When she finished strong, the audience clapped hard—though her parents praised her the loudest.

Why is it so hard to watch our children struggle and risk? We love them so much it feels our hearts could break, and yet somehow we know that while the stretching and reaching is risky, it is good. Can we protect *and* propel them to reach their highest potential? Our power as parents is just so...limited.

But God's isn't. There isn't a single molecule in our universe that doesn't submit to His authority. Like our children, we too take every breath by the power of His grace. And so we train and work and risk life in motion, knowing that even when we fall (what athlete doesn't?), our Sovereign Lord holds our hand. We may fear the failure, but God is forging character that winning alone can't wield. We trust His process, like a gymnast with her coach. And we keep our eyes focused on the stabilizing point of His sovereign presence.

THE LORD MAKES FIRM THE STEPS
OF THE ONE WHO DELIGHTS IN HIM;
THOUGH HE MAY STUMBLE, HE WILL NOT FALL,
FOR THE LORD UPHOLDS HIM WITH HIS HAND.
I WAS YOUNG AND NOW I AM OLD,
YET I HAVE NEVER SEEN THE RIGHTEOUS
FORSAKEN OR THEIR CHILDREN BEGGING BREAD.

PSALM 37:23–25 NIV

THE LOOK OF LOVE

*The Lord appeared to us
in the past, saying: "I have loved
you with an everlasting love;
I have drawn you with unfailing kindness."*

JEREMIAH 31:3 NIV

It's the moment you've been waiting for, and you're not willing for a single disruption to interrupt its impact. From the very first time they met, you knew this man and woman were made for each other. And as the story unfolded, you witnessed countless diversions and distractions that kept them from their divine destiny together. *When will they see the secret love we've understood all along?* we wonder. And wait.

And when it comes, our hearts explode in unexplained joy. *It's just a movie*, we remind ourselves, embarrassed a little by our unrestrained emotion. How can just a look of love—a first embrace—stir our souls so strongly?

By the warmth of such soul connection, our walls of self-protection crumble. For a moment we feel our vulnerability, the hint of hidden hope peeking through the rubble. *Will we ever be loved that way?* we dare to wonder.

Better than the best romance story ever told, we have a date with destiny—love's full expression still unfolding. In the waiting, though, we don't have to wonder. Jesus, our betrothed groom, has been preparing our miracle moment to be unveiled in face-to-face union with Him in heaven. We don't have to wander around this life wondering whether we'll ever be loved or chosen or whisked away to some wonderful place with our beloved. We will! Our hope has no need for fortress walls. Be bold, bride of Christ, and let God's love free you to revel in His divine pursuit and eternal affection for you.

....

WHOEVER DOES NOT LOVE
DOES NOT KNOW GOD,
BECAUSE GOD IS LOVE.

1 JOHN 4:8 NIV

STORYTELLING

Philip said, "Lord, show us the Father. That is all we need."
Jesus replied: "Philip, I have been with you for a long time.
Don't you know who I am? If you have seen Me, you have seen
the Father. How can you ask Me to show you the Father?"

JOHN 14:8–9 CEV

The children sat enthralled at the old man's feet. Occasionally his chair rocked back and forth as he waited for his last point to linger a little longer with his young listeners. Every story told blew their minds. And every week they gathered, eagerly awaiting the newest unveiling of intrigue. Full of unexpected twists and undeniable miracles, the old man painted his experiences in rural Uganda through truthful tales and vivid descriptions that sent their wildest imaginations soaring. There wasn't a child present who wasn't ready to go—right this minute—to experience the adventures for themselves.

And so is the nature of good storytelling. Unlike facts told in cold, hard prose, stories unfold in ways that unite our experience with imagination. Stories take what we know and lift our understanding beyond conventional boundaries to the land of endless possibilities. It's one of the reasons Jesus taught people in parables. But His greatest story takes us even higher.

More epic than the universe in which we live, we have a heavenly Father who wants us to know Him. But how could He show us a Spirit we can't see, whose essence is so "other" than any earthly father we've ever known? God painted the hues of His heart through the person of Jesus, God the Father expressed through the life story of His Son, Jesus.

Today, don't let the Father feel distant from you. With the faith of a wide-eyed child, come sit at the feet of our amazing Savior and revel in the Father's love as you realize your role in the greatest love adventure ever told.

•••••••••••••••••••••

SURELY YOU ARE STILL OUR FATHER!
EVEN IF ABRAHAM AND JACOB WOULD DISOWN US,
LORD, YOU WOULD STILL BE OUR FATHER.
YOU ARE OUR REDEEMER FROM AGES PAST.

ISAIAH 63:16 NLT

GUIDANCE COUNSELOR

For to us a child is born,
to us a Son is given,
and the government will be on His shoulders.
And He will be called
Wonderful Counselor, Mighty God,
Everlasting Father, Prince of Peace.

ISAIAH 9:6 NIV

She breathed in deeply and let out a sigh. With a touch of the screen, her phone conversation with her sister was over—for now. For years she had played the role of counselor, trying to bring calm to her sister's chaotic world. But her sister's impulsive choices and her endless stream of reckless relationships always sent her own emotions reeling. Like a stone in a rising river, she could feel the earth beneath her giving way. *How can I stay grounded when I'm always giving to others?* she wondered.

It's a question worth asking. After all, we have pressures of our own. Other people's problems simply compound the obvious issue: we need a helper. But who can handle—who even cares—about all the issues our hearts bear?

God.

The God who never sleeps or slumbers has His eyes on you and His heart toward you. As an ever-present Counselor, God's indwelling Spirit not only knows the way you work and think, but He sees into the hearts of the people you're trying to help. In amazing grace, He supplies the power and perspective we need to first receive God's grace and then to give it, time and time again.

Are you exhausted from your own servant heart, tired from the turmoil churning all around you? Don't grow weary in doing good, for you will reap a harvest if you don't give up. Instead, give in to the Spirit's counsel and let His power flow to others as your weakness forms the perfect channel for God's empowering grace.

· · · · · · · · · · · · · · · · · · · ·

THE ADVOCATE, THE HOLY SPIRIT, WHOM
THE FATHER WILL SEND IN MY NAME, WILL
TEACH YOU ALL THINGS AND WILL REMIND
YOU OF EVERYTHING I HAVE SAID TO YOU.

JOHN 14:26 NIV

NINJA WARRIORS

Whom have I in heaven but You?
And earth has nothing I desire besides You.
My flesh and my heart may fail,
but God is the strength of my heart
and my portion forever.

PSALM 73:25–26 NIV

It's fascinating, watching the nimble athletes maneuver across the Ninja Warrior obstacle course. Conscious of the ticking timer, each person strategizes the best way to attack the present challenge. Determination and focus fuse into an all-out effort to finish the course with the fastest time. Typically, no one has trouble with the first few events. But as the intensity drags on, their strength drains. Will they have what it takes to make it to the end?

The crowd cheers on each athlete because we see a little bit of ourselves in those Ninja Warrior wannabes. We may never have worked an obstacle course, but life itself is complicated enough. Every day we battle the brokenness we find in ourselves and the relationships around us. Just when we make it over one hurdle, we find ourselves facing what seems an insurmountable wall.

Will we have enough strength to finish the course? Or how about just the event in this moment?

It depends on our energy source. If we are working our way through life by our own willpower, pounding through every pressure in our own strength, we will get sapped. But we do have an endless source of strength in Jesus. Tap into the power of His Spirit by daily ingesting His words of life. Look to God in an attitude of constant prayer as you maneuver through your day. He alone has the strength and power to support you in the present life and the one to come. Plug into God's eternal strength, and He will make your path straight, your hands sure, your effort victorious.

* *

IT IS GOD WHO ARMS ME WITH STRENGTH
AND KEEPS MY WAY SECURE.

II SAMUEL 22:33 NIV

NO GOOD

Do not remember
the sins of my youth
and my rebellious ways;
according to Your love remember me,
for You, LORD, are good.

PSALM 25:7 NIV

You trusted him. Week after week you sat under his sermons, listening to your pastor pour out his heart along with powerful portions of God's Word. And even though he spoke of struggles, his admitted vulnerability only elevated him higher to "saint status" in your mind—until the story broke today, the headline alone breaking your heart. *How could he do that?* you gasp, as you read the scandalous report. Is there anyone good left in this world?

You don't have to wonder. Jesus already answered that question a long time ago. The man asking was a rich young ruler who wanted to know who qualified for heaven. "Have I been good enough?" he queried. Seeing into his soul, Jesus loved him AND pressed on his hidden problem to make the issue plain. Every person has a sin problem, except one. "No one is good—except God alone" (Mark 10:18 NIV). And, of course, He's right—because He's God.

As the body of Christ, we are called to work together for God's kingdom, but make no mistake: we still struggle with sin. Though God sees us as saints, covered by His Son, we still need our Savior every moment of the day. We wrestle with sin and rest in His grace together with others just like ourselves who need to know God's forgiveness and strength.

Don't let the misdeeds of others destroy your confidence in Christ. Instead, cling ever more closely to the only One who is truly good. He will give you the strength to stand and grace to catch you when you fall.

* * * * * * * * * * * * * * * * * * * *

DEAR FRIEND, DO NOT IMITATE WHAT IS EVIL BUT WHAT IS GOOD. ANYONE WHO DOES WHAT IS GOOD IS FROM GOD. ANYONE WHO DOES WHAT IS EVIL HAS NOT SEEN GOD.

III JOHN 1:11 NIV

WHISTLE-BLOWING

In fact, the reason I was born and came into the world is to testify to the truth. Everyone on the side of truth listens to Me.

JOHN 18:37 NIV

On the outside it looked like madness, and honestly some of the teachers would have agreed. "Whoever decided Field Day was a good idea must have been crazy," one joked to another. As the teachers looked out from their vantage point, hundreds of elementary students milled around on the grass, talking and playing. But with one long blow from the head teacher's whistle, the chaos came to an end. Every head turned; every eye looked to the one at the lead. They knew that if they wanted to get to play in this day's games, they'd better listen and do as she said.

The same is true for God's saints. On the surface, it can seem as if we're just one with the rest of the world, our worries and work no different from each other's. Turn on talk-show radio or the news and the chaos grows even louder, the conflicting opinions on what works best never-ending. Like the teachers on Field Day, it's enough to make anyone want to escape. Except we know the one with the whistle. If we want our day—our lives—to work, we'd do well to listen when He calls and walk the way He leads.

Jesus calms our chaos by the very essence of His nature. He doesn't just know the way to the truth; He IS the truth. And the Way to the Life He offers is available only for those who hear and heed His call to follow.

Amid the noisy clamor of our culture, will you tune in to the only source of Truth? Follow His voice alone to lead you away from all the madness to a life of meaning and joy in Him.

．．．．．．．．．．．．．．．．．．．．．．．

JESUS ANSWERED, "I AM THE WAY AND THE TRUTH AND THE LIFE. NO ONE COMES TO THE FATHER EXCEPT THROUGH ME."

JOHN 14:6 NIV

LIFE LIGHT

Jesus said to her, "I am the resurrection and the life. The one
who believes in Me will live, even though they die; and whoever
lives by believing in Me will never die. Do you believe this?"
"Yes, Lord," she replied, "I believe that You are the Messiah,
the Son of God, who is to come into the world."

JOHN 11:25–27 NIV

They had sent for help long before Lazarus breathed his last
breaths. The sisters watched their brother's life ebb away,
wondering all the while, *Where is Jesus?*

Four days Lazarus lay in the grave, rotting. It was all ruined.
It's no wonder Mary didn't come running when she heard her
Lord had finally arrived in town. But Martha did, greeting him
at the village gate. Full of questions, she stopped short at His.
"I am the resurrection and the life," Jesus declared. "Do you
believe this?"

Did she hear the Rabbi right? Did this man before her eyes
really have the power to resurrect the dead? Though her mind
answered in the affirmative, Jesus continued His path to her
heart. "Show me where your hope died," He prompted. "If you
believe, you'll see God's glory there."

Practical Martha protested. "He's too far gone now, Lord. The dead just stink too much!"

Her perception didn't fully estimate God's power. Pushing past the mourning people with tears of His own streaming down His face, Jesus looked at the sealed grave. Then He shouted, "Lazarus, come forth!" As Lazarus obeyed, hope was reborn, the now-empty tomb an unquestionable triumph. Seeing became true believing, and their hearts rejoiced with hope.

Believer, Jesus is our life, too. He calls us to come forth from our places of despair and witness the wonder of His power and love. Like Lazarus, we must come to the end of ourselves to see and believe in the resurrection power of God.

• • • • • • • • • • • • • • • • • • • •

WHEN JESUS SPOKE AGAIN TO THE PEOPLE, HE SAID, "I AM THE LIGHT OF THE WORLD. WHOEVER FOLLOWS ME WILL NEVER WALK IN DARKNESS, BUT WILL HAVE THE LIGHT OF LIFE."

JOHN 8:12 NIV

I AM ALWAYS

He said to me: "It is done. I am the Alpha and the Omega,
the Beginning and the End. To the thirsty I will give water
without cost from the spring of the water of life."
REVELATION 21:6 NIV

M a'am, do you know who's responsible for this?" asked a
stern, concerned police officer, standing beside the broken wall and the wreck that is your car. You wish you could
say, "No, I have no idea." Or at least point the finger in some
other likely direction. But you were texting, and there really is
no other explanation. "Yes, officer," you choke on the words.
"I am." With two little words, the whole weight of the world
seems to fall on your shoulders.

But what if the tables were turned? What if the officer said
instead, "I am taking care of all this"? Would you not wonder at
his generosity and grapple with such unexpected mercy? With
a deep sigh of relief, you'd likely shower your hero with deep
and heartfelt gratitude.

As unlikely as such a scenario seems, a similar shift happens
to us under the shadow of the Almighty. Culpable though we
are, God offers to cover our offenses at all cost to Himself.

In the exchange, our burdens are lifted onto the One whose shoulders are broad enough to bear them. The two little words "I AM" take on much more impact. For everything we owe and all that we need to carry on in this life and the next, God declares, "I am."

And He is. Our God is the great I Am who always was, still is, and forever will be. Rest as you realize, "I Am your righteousness. I Am your hope. I Am your peace. And I Am—always."

* * *

"VERY TRULY I TELL YOU,"
JESUS ANSWERED, "BEFORE
ABRAHAM WAS BORN, I AM!"

JOHN 8:58 NIV

RICH REWARD

I say to myself, "The LORD is my portion;
therefore I will wait for Him."
LAMENTATIONS 3:24 NIV

The candles are burning low," the wedding director whispered to the young bride's mom. Since early that morning, the flowers had all been perfectly placed, the chairs lined up along the lake's shore. Prepared food filled the warming ovens, ready for the reception soon to take place—surely.

"Should we at least go ahead and start the music?" the bride's mom asked in return.

But the bride overheard and held her voice firm. "What good is a wedding without the groom? We will wait for him."

In any situation, waiting is work. In the interim between hope and fulfillment lie all the what-ifs: What if it doesn't work out? What if no one ever comes? What if I've been fooled? What if…

But what if the reward comes in portions greater than our grandest expectations? What if waiting only deepens our desire?

Believers, why do we insist on running ahead of our Savior? What can we work out ourselves without the Person whose presence is the very point of our existence? Let your fears go as you focus on the faithful One. Take time before the day's hurry begins and talk to your Father. Listen for His voice and praise Him for His promises. Though He may tarry, your groom will pull through—the power of His presence your richest reward for your wait.

* *

DO NOT BE AFRAID, ABRAM.
I AM YOUR SHIELD,
YOUR VERY GREAT REWARD.

GENESIS 15:1 NIV

SHOWING UP

In your relationships with one another, have
the same mindset as Christ Jesus:
Who, being in very nature God,
did not consider equality with God something
to be used to His own advantage;
rather, He made Himself nothing
by taking the very nature of a servant.

PHILIPPIANS 2:5–7 NIV

A reality show currently airs on TV, featuring a different major-corporation CEO per episode. In each episode, the business owner ditches his white-collar suit to don the common laborer's clothes. No one announces anything to the workers. He simply shows up as one of them, seeking to learn the skills of their trade. Hidden cameras record the whole exchange, including the honest conversation that comes when working alongside one another. And it is brutally honest. In the interactions, disloyal and lazy attitudes often surface, while other employees reveal a strong work ethic. In the end, when the owner's true identity is revealed, each worker reaps what their attitudes earned, while the owner now runs his business with greater empathy for those who work under him.

Why does the trick work every time? Because no one expects the owner to appear as a common laborer. Yet God, creator, owner, and sustainer of the entire universe, came to earth—not for a simple show but to live a lifetime in our shoes. In astonishing humility, He even arrived in the poorest of places, not seeking to assert power and prestige but to learn obedience through service and suffering.

The humility of Christ helps us to rest. We have no need to put on airs because our Savior donned a servant's towel to wash dirty feet and show us a greater way.

············

HE HAS SHOWN YOU, O MORTAL, WHAT IS GOOD. AND WHAT DOES THE LORD REQUIRE OF YOU? TO ACT JUSTLY AND TO LOVE MERCY AND TO WALK HUMBLY WITH YOUR GOD.

MICAH 6:8 NIV

DELIVERANCE

One of you routs a thousand, because the LORD
your God fights for you, just as He promised.
JOSHUA 23:10 NIV

Elisha's servant stood frozen in fear. Everywhere he and Elisha looked, they saw enemy soldiers encircling their city. "There must be thousands here," the servant said, starting to panic. But Elisha stood in perfect peace. What was the difference?

Elisha's perspective. The two men saw the same situation through very different lenses. So Elisha prayed for his servant—and God opened his eyes. More numerous than the enemy soldiers, God's mighty army surrounded Elisha and his servant for protection, blazing chariots included. The servant's quaking heart surged with confidence. Strangely, instead of using swords to fight, Elisha simply prayed that God would blind his enemies. Suddenly they didn't know where they were, and Elisha led them to a distant town!

It's just one of many victory stories the Bible records where God came to the rescue in the most unconventional way. In some of their conquests, they were required to circle Jericho for seven days in silence, shouting on the last day to bring the walls down. In another battle they smashed clay jars at God's command and startled their enemy into a self-killing frenzy. No matter which way God chose to deliver His people and no matter how small their numbers, God's people won every time they obeyed His commands.

The same God who worked wonders then still stands in command now. Heaven's armies are also at our disposal, ready to defeat our opposition as we fall in line with God's kingdom work. So what kind of foe opposes you today? How bleak does the outlook appear? Like Elisha, pray for clearer sight so you can see God's delivering power at work. When we trust God to fight our battles for us, we find the sweetest and most surprising victories.

●●●●●●●●●●●●●●●●●●●●●

THE ENEMY TOOK THEM AS PRISONERS.
AND THEY WON'T LET THEM GO.
BUT GOD IS STRONG AND WILL BUY THEM BACK.
HIS NAME IS THE LORD OF HEAVEN'S ARMIES.
HE WILL DEFEND THEM WITH POWER
SO HE CAN GIVE REST TO THEIR LAND.

JEREMIAH 50:33–34 ICB

TALK IT OUT

Come now, let us reason together, says the LORD:
though your sins are like scarlet,
they shall be as white as snow;
though they are red like crimson,
they shall become like wool.

ISAIAH 1:18 ESV

She knew it was over for her the minute those blue swirling lights appeared in the driveway. The party had started calmly enough, just a few of her teenaged friends hanging out while parents were elsewhere. She wasn't even sure who brought whatever it was that she drank; she just knew that when the police arrived, she had no strength to run like many of the rest. When her parents came to take her home, she had no words to say.

But they did! When her mind finally cleared, they called her in to talk it out. Consequences would be doled out, but they were most concerned with her heart. Had she learned a lesson? Would she leave behind her careless, foolish ways?

With a similar tone, our heavenly Father wants to work with us, wayward children that we often are. Far from the often-held image of fearful judge, God calls us to Himself as our loving, concerned Father. He wants to reason together: Are we really headed the way we want to go? Will we reconsider a better path that leads away from pain to peace?

When we surrender to our Father in repentance, our acts of aggression are covered in forgiveness. He doesn't hold grudges or keep long lists of grievances. God separates our sins from us as far as the east stays away from the west. In repentance, we find rest in the mercy of our gracious Father.

THE LORD HAS MERCY ON THOSE
WHO FEAR HIM, AS A FATHER HAS
MERCY ON HIS CHILDREN.

PSALM 103:13 ICB

PAINTING GRACE

He chose us in him before the creation of the world
to be holy and blameless in His sight. In love He
predestined us for adoption to sonship through Jesus
Christ, in accordance with His pleasure and will.

EPHESIANS 1:4–5 NIV

The artist surveyed his empty canvas. Though only white gesso coated the surface, the colors and shapes of a finished work formed solidly in his mind. And so he set to work, stroke after stroke, bleeding some colors and carving out others. While in process, the placement of hues and shapes seemed pointless. But at his completion, his plan for a beautiful portrait was perfectly clear.

It is amazing to watch a skilled artist at work. How does he get the image in his head to emerge with such dimension on a dull, flat board? We could ask our heavenly Father the same question. More skilled than any earthly artist, God has preplanned each of His children, choosing our shape and form, crafting us for our life's calling before He colored in a single stroke of our lives. With strategic precision, God plotted and framed the very family into which we were born. Using shadows and light,

He shaped our personalities, minds, and physical features that we see with eyes that He made in just the right shade. No part of who we are or the lives we live unfold by accident. For those who love God, every part works together into the wonderful masterpiece our Author has planned.

When you look at yourself, do you like what you see? We find rest when we remember we are God's work in process. As we surrender to each stroke, we watch a supernatural creativity carve amazing depth and beauty into the canvas of our lives.

....

LISTEN TO ME, YOU ISLANDS;
HEAR THIS, YOU DISTANT NATIONS:
BEFORE I WAS BORN THE LORD CALLED ME;
FROM MY MOTHER'S WOMB
HE HAS SPOKEN MY NAME.

ISAIAH 49:1 NIV

SOUL SURGERY

He heals the brokenhearted
and binds up their wounds.
PSALM 147:3 NIV

The procedure sounded terrifying. "It's just a simple cut across the surface of each eye," the ophthalmologist explained. "Then we just shine a laser light in for a few minutes and it'll all be done." The young patient calculated her options. Gut instinct told her to cut and run. How could razors and eyeballs ever be a good combination? But on the other hand, she could barely see without her glasses, and her dog always had a hankering for some good, expensive eyewear. On the front end, Lasik surgery seemed like so much risk. But in the end, she put her sight in the surgeon's hands—and her life has never been the same. "Everything looks so amazingly clear to me now!" she beams, beckoning others to experience the same healing for themselves.

And so it is with our Savior. We hear Him say, "Give up your life in exchange for Mine," and we worry about the risk. Maybe our broken, sin-sick lives aren't so bad after all, we hedge, hoping to avoid unwanted soul surgery. Perhaps we can get by with some self-applied bandages. But to resist His hand means to remain unhealed. Or as the Bible says: in keeping our life, we lose it. Our condition is far worse than simple sickness. Our spirits are dead and need a resurrection.

When we realize the gravity of our situation, our desperation drives us to the Healer. But take courage! He specializes in the brokenhearted and brings a clarity to our life's purpose we would have never thought possible.

········

"BUT IF YOU CAN DO ANYTHING,
TAKE PITY ON US AND HELP US."
"'IF YOU CAN'?" SAID JESUS. "EVERYTHING
IS POSSIBLE FOR ONE WHO BELIEVES."
IMMEDIATELY THE BOY'S FATHER
EXCLAIMED, "I DO BELIEVE; HELP ME
OVERCOME MY UNBELIEF!"

MARK 9:22-24 NIV

TRASH DAY

As far as the east is from the west, so far has
He removed our transgressions from us.
PSALM 103:12 NIV

As soon as she stepped inside the house, she could smell it. "What is that awful stench?" she called aloud, hoping in vain that her kids could give her a clue. So she began the sleuthing process, searching and sniffing the pantry, the laundry, and all the other places that could potentially put out such putrid fumes.

And then she found it.

Tucked away in the corner of her garage, something noxious was growing inside the large blue trash bin. "Thank the Lord tomorrow's trash day!" she mumbled to herself as she wheeled the bin to the curb. And when she awoke the next morning, no trace of her trash remained.

Do you treasure your trash service? Maybe you've never thought about it—at least until it fails to show up for some reason. When trash starts to pile up, we start to panic. "How do I get this stuff out of here?"

Strangely, trash day helps us picture our soul situation better. Without God's amazing grace, we're stuck in the growing stench of all our various sins. As they pile up, we start to worry, *Who else can smell the muck I live in?* If we want to rest and breathe easy, we just need to bring our junk out in the open where God will remove it, never to reach us again. Why wait another minute? The moment we turn to God in repentance, our sin's stench disappears.

IF WE CONFESS OUR SINS,
HE IS FAITHFUL AND JUST AND WILL
FORGIVE US OUR SINS AND PURIFY US
FROM ALL UNRIGHTEOUSNESS.

I JOHN 1:9 NIV

SINGLED OUT

This is what the Lord says—
He who created you, Jacob,
He who formed you, Israel:
"Do not fear, for I have redeemed you;
I have summoned you by name; you are Mine....
Since you are precious
and honored in My sight,
and because I love you,
I will give people in exchange for you,
nations in exchange for your life.

ISAIAH 43:1, 4 NIV

Arriving early as usual, the young intern flipped the switch and lit up the small room full of office cubicles. Just the steady hum of the copier warming up broke the calm quiet as she rounded the corner to her small desk—the place where people higher up than her often dumped the tedious work they'd rather have her do.

But today was different. Paper stars cut out by hand lined her wall. Small streamers dangled from her cubby bin. And a flowing spray of fragrant flowers filled the space where her day's work usually went. Alongside it, a note said simply, "You are a sensational star on our team. Today, we celebrate you!"

She didn't know what to say. Somebody had taken the time to do this. Suddenly she felt seen. Known. And loved—exactly what they wanted her to feel.

At the heart of all good gifts lies a celebration of the one who's loved. Singled out from the masses, we feel important to someone.

You, child of God, have been singled out this day—and every day. As you make the rounds of your regular routine, do you see God's celebration? It's written in His Word and the way He calls you by name. It's painted in the skies at sunrise and shouted in the colorful clouds at dusk. Your God delights in you. He sees you, knows you, and sings over the sensational person He's made you to be. Don't miss the moment—or any of the daily reminders He tucks away in your day. Today, live as you are loved because you are.

GIVE EAR AND COME TO ME; LISTEN, THAT YOU MAY LIVE. I WILL MAKE AN EVERLASTING COVENANT WITH YOU, MY FAITHFUL LOVE PROMISED TO DAVID.

ISAIAH 55:3 NIV

DRESSED FOR SUCCESS

May Your priests be clothed with Your righteousness;
may Your faithful people sing for joy.
PSALM 132:9 NIV

The moment she walked through the doorway, she knew she'd missed the memo. "Look at how everyone's dressed!" She elbowed her date, who had failed to relate the invitation details. Her favorite jeans and T-shirt, a suitable selection for other occasions, made her feel humiliated in front of everyone wearing floor-length gowns and black-tie tuxedos. Underdressed and overwhelmed, she simply wanted to leave. "We just don't fit in here," she hissed, pulling her apologetic date back out.

It's funny how something as simple as clothes affects our feelings of security. When we look smart or at least fit the part, we feel more like we belong.

Surprisingly, there's something deeper than social conventions in what could seem strictly superficial. Spiritually speaking, clothes do make the man—and woman. But not the kind with designer labels or intricate designs. From the days back in the Garden, we've all had a garment problem, trying to cover our inadequacies with whatever type of fig leaf we can find.

But God won't have it. His children dress in His royal best. So He provides the robes. Just as He clothed Adam and Eve with a more permanent covering, He clothes each child of God in the righteousness of His Son. We can't be a part of His family without it. But wrapped in God's favor and made right through our Savior, we are at home wherever His family gathers.

Do you feel "less than" when you're around certain others? Remember, you are clothed in God's permanent affection, and your presence is needed at the party!

• •

I SAW THE HOLY CITY, THE NEW JERUSALEM,
COMING DOWN OUT OF HEAVEN FROM
GOD, PREPARED AS A BRIDE BEAUTIFULLY
DRESSED FOR HER HUSBAND.

REVELATION 21:2 NIV

LIONHEART

The Spirit God gave us does not make us timid,
but gives us power, love and self-discipline.
II TIMOTHY 1:7 NIV

You could say she was a closet pray-er. Daily she prayed for her family, friends, and neighbors—especially the ones she knew hadn't yet surrendered to Jesus. On her knees in her bedroom, she was bold before the throne of God, asking for opportunities to share God's love with others.

But once she left the comfort of her own familiar quarters, she felt the battle begin. Out in the world where the people she prayed for lived, she felt less certain. For years she had simply blamed her inhibition on her temperament type. After all, the test profile proved that she was an introvert. So naturally, the way she avoided conversation, especially about her Christianity, was just a funny facet of the personality God had given her.

But no psychology test tells the full story for a believer. Ordinary inhibitions submit to God's supernatural power as we surrender to Him. No matter what our personality type may be, God gives us all a holy boldness when we seek His face first and fuel our faith with His truth and presence.

Insecurities about our own abilities to carry out Jesus's Great Commission only open the door for God to do what we in our own strength can't.

Instead of cowering, cutting off the potential for spiritual conversation, trust God to make you brave and bold as a lion. As we pray, watch, and anticipate God moving, we can rest from our worries as we watch God make bold evangelists out of us all.

....

THE WICKED FLEE THOUGH
NO ONE PURSUES,
BUT THE RIGHTEOUS
ARE AS BOLD AS A LION.

PROVERBS 28:1 NIV

MIXED WITH LOVE

For I am convinced that neither death nor life, neither angels nor demons, neither the present nor the future, nor any powers, neither height nor depth, nor anything else in all creation, will be able to separate us from the love of God that is in Christ Jesus our Lord.

ROMANS 8:38–39 NIV

As the porch swing gently swayed, the little girl looked up at her daddy's face, her own full of concern. "Daddy, will you ever stop loving me?" she wondered.

"No, honey, I'll always love you," he replied.

"But what if I do something really, really bad? Will you stop loving me then?" she tested.

He tipped his face in her direction. "Do me a favor," he said. "Would you please take your glass of lemonade and separate the ingredients? I want my lemons, sugar, and water separate."

Confused, she answered, "Well, I can't do that, Daddy. Once they're mixed, you can't unmix it!"

"And that's how it is with my love for the one." He smiled.

It's no wonder in our world that we worry about our relationships. Some of the simplest conflicts can cause so much division that decades go by before any resolution is made. We often hide the truth of who we are inside for fear that those we love will leave us if they knew.

But God's love for us is far different from what we find in this world. Once God has added His love to the mix in our lives, we are an entirely new creation—one that can never go back to the life we knew before. No matter what our failures and frailties may be, our heavenly Father relentlessly loves us. Without any fear of present or future rejection, we are free to rest in real, authentic relationship with God.

●●●●●●●●●●●●●●●●●●●●●●

THOUGH THE MOUNTAINS BE SHAKEN
AND THE HILLS BE REMOVED,
YET MY UNFAILING LOVE
FOR YOU WILL NOT BE SHAKEN
NOR MY COVENANT
OF PEACE BE REMOVED,"
SAYS THE LORD, WHO HAS
COMPASSION ON YOU.

ISAIAH 54:10 NIV

91

ALL THIS WAY

There is no fear in love. But perfect love drives out
fear, because fear has to do with punishment. The
one who fears is not made perfect in love.
We love because He first loved us.

I JOHN 4:18–19 NIV

He thought he was too late. A series of misunderstandings and missed opportunities had led their blooming love down different paths. Now she had flown away and settled on a far distant shore, certain he didn't care about her anymore... until she heard the knock. Opening her door, she gasped in amazement. *He came all this way!* His pursuit proved the love she longed for to be true. "Dreams really do come true," she whispered when they embraced.

And they do. Not just in the movies, but in the here and now. Deep within our souls, we feel the ache of separation caused by sin in this world. We want to feel unfettered affection, the kind that values us enough to push past our defenses to see us and love us for who we truly are. But does anyone actually do that?

God does. He loves us with an everlasting love. Though our sin has separated us and sent us to the farthest corners of our souls in opposition to His holiness, He has come after us. He left heaven to seek us out and even suffer a horrific death just to save our lives. Best of all, He's risen again and has promised to return one glorious day for all His people. We're never left to wonder whether our God still loves us. *He came all this way!* And He stands knocking on the door of our lives, waiting for us to let Him in and enjoy the eternal rest in His love.

• •

I TOOK YOU FROM THE ENDS OF THE EARTH, FROM ITS FARTHEST CORNERS I CALLED YOU. I SAID, "YOU ARE MY SERVANT"; I HAVE CHOSEN YOU AND HAVE NOT REJECTED YOU."

ISAIAH 41:9 NIV

REMEMBERED

*Can a mother forget
the baby at her breast
and have no compassion
on the child she has borne?
Though she may forget,
I will not forget you!
See, I have engraved you
on the palms of My hands;
your walls are ever before Me.*

ISAIAH 49:15–16 NIV

"Can you take my picture?" she asked, wanting to be remembered as having attended the party. Her family members smiled and nodded, knowing her needs. From as long as anyone could remember, she brought her camera everywhere. In fact, they often wondered whether she saw more of the world through her camera lens than with her own eyes. But she was driven to capture moments, haunted by the fear that one day she'd forget. Worse yet, that others would forget she'd been there.

After all, who wants to be forgotten? Don't we all work hard to build the kinds of connections that can keep that from ever happening? We spend all our money, effort, and time trying to make our time here matter, so maybe someone will notice—and remember. And even after all our efforts, we still worry and wonder whether it is enough.

But God puts our fears to rest. Knowing our need for assurance, He has taken the matter into His own hands quite literally, etching our names onto His eternal palms. He has captured us—in all our lives' earthly brevity—and bound us together with all the importance and power of His eternal presence. Our moments in life matter not because others remember what we've done, but because our loving God never forgets His children.

Today, take comfort in God's watchful care, knowing that your every move is on His loving mind. You matter to God, and He will direct your steps to work out His wonderful, meaningful, and eternal purpose for this day.

GOD—HIS WAY IS PERFECT;
THE WORD OF THE LORD IS PURE.
HE IS A SHIELD TO ALL
WHO TAKE REFUGE IN HIM.

PSALM 18:30 CSB

DAILY DRILLS

Have you completely forgotten this word of encouragement
that addresses you as a father addresses his son? It says, "My
son, do not make light of the Lord's discipline, and do not lose
heart when He rebukes you, because the Lord disciplines the one
He loves, and He chastens everyone He accepts as His son."

HEBREWS 12:5–6 NIV

The young athlete's confusion soon turned to anger toward his coach. *I didn't sign up for this mess!* he thought as he recalled the week's practice out on the hot field. Even though he had been a top prospect for most of the country, he had chosen this program because he'd heard it was the best. But ever since he got there, the coach had seemed anything but kind. When he ran drills, the coach made him run farther, faster, and harder than anyone else on the team.

"What kind of treatment is this?" he finally complained to his coach.

The reply came quickly, "The kind I only give athletes with real potential!"

Good players know that without correction and driving discipline, they won't rise to the top of their game. But somehow

Christians often lose the connection in the spiritual world. All of God's promises of love and peace get misperceived as guarantees against pain and suffering in this world. But Jesus corrects the judgment error. "You will have trouble in this world," He assures us. But we take heart because He has overcome it! (See John 16:33.)

Trials in this life become tools to sharpen us where we need skill training the most. When life doesn't go as planned or you find yourself in a place of suffering, don't wonder what you did wrong to deserve this treatment. Instead, submit your life to His loving leadership. Let His Spirit work in you the kind of character building that only comes from a good Father.

•••••••••••••••••••••

THEY DISCIPLINED US FOR A LITTLE WHILE AS THEY THOUGHT BEST; BUT GOD DISCIPLINES US FOR OUR GOOD, IN ORDER THAT WE MAY SHARE IN HIS HOLINESS.

HEBREWS 12:10 NIV

ROYAL BLOOD

There is surely a future hope for you,
and your hope will not be cut off.
PROVERBS 23:18 NIV

To the young child, it was just another day of homeschool. Within the castle walls he learned to build with blocks, write the alphabet, and paint the kind of pictures typical for someone his age. So why were so many reporters clamoring in the hallway outside his classroom, commentating on his every action? Why was so much attention directed toward one child and his ordinary day?

He was no ordinary child. The young prince would one day become king. And everyone around him understood his destiny far better than he did. Even mundane activities took on greater meaning with his ultimate destiny in mind. They marveled at his royal training and wondered what it was like to be born into greatness.

Truth be told, angels could identify with those reporters. Created by God to guard His people, the Bible says they watch and marvel as our lives unfold. *What must it be like to be adopted into God's royal family?* they wonder. *How must it feel to live so loved as God's precious children?* They long to understand the life of glory and affection we live.

Yet often we are like the young prince, unaware of our declared destiny. We go about our day as if it's like any other, not realizing the King of glory has planned every moment for our training and tutelage until we will one day reign with Jesus!

If you belong to Christ, your coronation day is coming. Keep your eyes on kingdom work and train well with eternal purpose, princes and princesses of the King!

....

AS IT IS WRITTEN:
"WHAT NO EYE HAS SEEN,
WHAT NO EAR HAS HEARD,
AND WHAT NO HUMAN MIND
HAS CONCEIVED"—
THE THINGS GOD HAS PREPARED
FOR THOSE WHO LOVE HIM.

I CORINTHIANS 2:9 NIV

TRAVEL PLANS

This is what the LORD says—
your Redeemer, who formed you in the womb:
I am the LORD, the Maker of all things,
who stretches out the heavens,
who spreads out the earth by Myself.

ISAIAH 44:24 NIV

It was just a pinprick in the distance, but you were delighted, knowing it was now only a short drive away. "Kids, it's time to wake up!" you called with enthusiasm. For months you had planned and plotted each point of interest you wanted your family to experience in Yellowstone National Park. And to ensure that everything went as smoothly as possible, you went ahead and assigned special tasks for each person. By working together as a team, everyone would get to eat, share the hiking-gear load, and enjoy time together at each spectacular point along the way.

In a similar way, our heavenly Father has planned the trip of a lifetime for each one of His kids, our final destination more spectacular than all the earthbound natural wonders combined. But reaching the end isn't the only objective.

There's plenty of beauty to behold along the way—traveling as a team. We go as a family, working together to make travel lighter and paths clearer, and to help troubleshoot any obstacles we encounter along the way. In fact, our Father has crafted each of His kids with unique abilities perfectly designed to work best with all the others in order to experience the adventure of a lifetime.

Today, thank God for your special calling, and seek His wisdom to know it and walk in it. Rest from the temptation to carry out tasks assigned to other team members. Together, we will watch God's kingdom unfold in beautiful scenes of grace all along the path to glory.

* * *

FOR WE ARE GOD'S HANDIWORK,
CREATED IN CHRIST JESUS
TO DO GOOD WORKS,
WHICH GOD PREPARED
IN ADVANCE FOR US TO DO.

EPHESIANS 2:10 NIV

MAKING AMENDS

All of this is a gift from God, who brought us back to Himself through Christ. And God has given us this task of reconciling people to Him. For God was in Christ, reconciling the world to Himself, no longer counting people's sins against them. And He gave us this wonderful message of reconciliation. So we are Christ's ambassadors; God is making His appeal through us. We speak for Christ when we plead, "Come back to God!"

II CORINTHIANS 5:18–20 NLT

When the teen stormed off to her room and slammed the door, both parents looked at each other and sighed. "She can be so stubborn!" her mom said under her breath. But then she went to her daughter's door and knocked on it lightly anyway.

"Honey, can I talk to you?" she asked. She had no idea whether her words could help bring down her daughter's walls, but it was worth a shot. More than anything in this moment, her mom knew she needed friends who loved her—even if they were her parents!

Whether out in the world or inside our own homes, people of all ages feel the effects of sin—including the broken relationships and fractured hope rising from it. And Christians aren't immune, either. We all have an enemy whose primary aim is to divide and conquer, suffocating our hope and joy in the process. Polarizing political views, differing denominations, and dividing families are simply some of his favorite ways to tear us apart.

But we have a heavenly Father in the reconciliation business. As His children, we've taken up the trade as well. By His Spirit, we are called to keep reaching out in love, our intent to reconcile the lost with God. We don't give up and we don't give in to despair or hopeless thinking, because God's heart for reconciliation reigns with power within us.

Who today needs to hear His heart? Ask God to make your path plain and your conversation full of His Spirit.

●●●●●●●●●●●●●●●●●●●●●●

WHEN I BRING YOU BACK, PEOPLE WILL SAY, "THIS FORMER WASTELAND IS NOW LIKE THE GARDEN OF EDEN! THE ABANDONED AND RUINED CITIES NOW HAVE STRONG WALLS AND ARE FILLED WITH PEOPLE!"

EZEKIEL 36:35 NLT

RISING UP

Now He uses us to spread the knowledge of Christ everywhere,
like a sweet perfume. Our lives are a Christ-like fragrance
rising up to God. But this fragrance is perceived differently by
those who are being saved and by those who are perishing.

II CORINTHIANS 2:14–15 NLT

As she walked into the clothing store, she couldn't keep her eyes off the life-sized photos lining the wall. Every one of them depicted a beautiful (and of course skinny) girl with some gorgeous guy, laughing and living the good life. The room itself smelled like romance—and rich living. Mesmerized by every incoming sensation, she decided, *I want that! Why can't that be me?*

The marketing worked well by design. Our culture caters to our desire for connection, intimacy, and importance. If advertisers do their job well enough, we'll shell out whatever it takes to have their piece of promised happiness.

Only it's hollow. The pleasure it provides passes so quickly, we wonder what happened.

When the deception is realized, we reel with disappointment and disillusionment and, ultimately, a desire for more, mistakenly thinking that *this time* it will last. Deep within, we know it won't.

But God's marketing plan is markedly different. He doesn't post billboards about the abundant life He offers; He puts His Spirit inside His believers! As we walk around our homes, workplaces, and even favorite vacation spots, we emit the unusual fragrance of purpose and authenticity blended with love that lasts forever. As people see us spreading God's truth through acts of love, they smell the distinction between us and the world. The scent of God's Spirit always wields impact: to the rebellious, it repulses; but to the dying and desperate, it's the refreshing fragrance of renewal and hope.

••••••••••••••••••••••

LIVE A LIFE FILLED WITH LOVE, FOLLOWING
THE EXAMPLE OF CHRIST. HE LOVED US
AND OFFERED HIMSELF AS A SACRIFICE
FOR US, A PLEASING AROMA TO GOD.

EPHESIANS 5:2 NLT

REACHING OUT

*God is able to bless you abundantly, so that in
all things at all times, having all that you need,
you will abound in every good work.*

II CORINTHIANS 9:8 NIV

As she went to get her mail, the young lady looked wistfully down the street. A couple of doors down, her newly widowed neighbor stood peering into her own mailbox. Their eyes met. There was a pause. An awkward wave and a smile ensued, with the obligatory "Hello, how are you?" Retreating quickly inside, the young Christian woman chided herself the whole way. *I should reach out to her,* her mind scolded. *I should say something, do something—but...* And then a litany of rational reasons of why she should keep her distance dominated her good idea.

Unfortunately, our enemy uses two powerful weapons to prevent us from successful connection. First, he turns our focus on our inadequacies and past rejections. Adding insult to injury, he heaps on guilt when we fail to follow through, keeping the vicious cycle of fear and self-doubt repeating, instead of allowing us to reach out for meaningful relationships.

But God made us for so much more! We don't need to second-guess ourselves or strategize every ministry event. We simply surrender to God's Spirit inside us, knowing that He will not only guide us to every good work, but He'll supply the right words to say when we need them. Even as we walk toward opportunity, we rest knowing God will handle the results!

Today, ask God to open doors and make you brave to share with those around you. When you see the moment arise, sense God's Spirit surging inside you with His boldness and love. God will lead you and grow your faith in the following.

PRAY FOR US, TOO, THAT GOD MAY OPEN A DOOR FOR OUR MESSAGE, SO THAT WE MAY PROCLAIM THE MYSTERY OF CHRIST.

COLOSSIANS 4:3 NIV

CALMING WORDS

Have I not commanded you? Be strong and courageous.
Do not be afraid; do not be discouraged, for the LORD
your God will be with you wherever you go.

JOSHUA 1:9 NIV

She woke up with a feeling of dread. The day had finally arrived. No amount of planning or plotting could stall the inevitable any longer—and she wondered how she'd even make it out of bed, let alone face all that she knew lay ahead.

But as the early morning light slowly peeked through her shades, another thought dawned and she picked up her Bible beside the bed. There, in the pages of God's Word, she saw the promise. Written in red, Jesus's words proclaimed, "Surely I am with you always, to the very end of the age" (Matthew 28:20 NIV).

What a promise! No matter what kind of darkness threatens to undo us, we live with the promise that God never leaves us. As Jesus demonstrated to His disciples, He remains calm and completely in control of even the wildest storms. When we believe in God's goodness and power to save, our souls settle into rest with Him as we wait for His authoritative Word to have its way in our harrowing moments. Every turbulent time is an amazing opportunity to see how our Savior is mighty enough to save—*even in this*. Without the storm, we'd never experience His life-changing presence in its midst.

Instead of dreading our darkest hours or demanding that they end, draw closer to the Lord. Take pleasure in His presence and authority over your situation, and enter His rest knowing that you are safest by His side.

I HAVE RESCUED YOU.
I HAVE CALLED YOU BY NAME;
NOW YOU BELONG TO ME.
WHEN YOU CROSS DEEP RIVERS,
I WILL BE WITH YOU,
AND YOU WON'T DROWN.
WHEN YOU WALK THROUGH FIRE,
YOU WON'T BE BURNED
OR SCORCHED BY THE FLAMES.
I AM THE LORD, YOUR GOD,
THE HOLY ONE OF ISRAEL,
THE GOD WHO SAVES YOU.

ISAIAH 43:1–3 CEV

PURCHASE RECEIPT

He has identified us as His own by placing the Holy
Spirit in our hearts as the first installment that
guarantees everything He has promised us.
II CORINTHIANS 1:22 NLT

As she pushed her shopping cart slowly down the aisle, she scanned each shelf. So many variables factored into her thinking, but she wanted to get the best bang for her buck. Occasionally she'd find a better deal a little farther down and return her original choice to its spot. She proceeded this way throughout the store until she was finished, ready to make her final purchase, satisfied that she had selected well.

Sometimes, if we're honest, we harbor a secret fear inside. We see our position as Christians a little like those items the lady stored in her shopping cart. Sure, we're doing okay right now, but what if we screw something up or someone better comes along, and God puts us back? Just how certain can we be that we'll reach the final register to be purchased permanently?

Before we were even born, God knew the insecurities that would lurk in our hearts. So He gave us a picture to adjust our thinking. Even though we haven't yet reached heaven,

God provides a guarantee that His children will all get there. When we come to Jesus by faith, the purchase transaction is complete—and comes with a receipt. God's own Spirit fills our hearts, permanently planted in the new creation of who we are. He's not going anywhere without us. From now until we reach eternity's shore, we rest in the hope of all God's promises, proven by the presence of His Spirit in us.

THE SPIRIT IS GOD'S GUARANTEE THAT HE WILL GIVE US THE INHERITANCE HE PROMISED AND THAT HE HAS PURCHASED US TO BE HIS OWN PEOPLE. HE DID THIS SO WE WOULD PRAISE AND GLORIFY HIM.

EPHESIANS 1:14 NLT

LOADED

I pray that the eyes of your heart may be enlightened in
order that you may know the hope to which He has called
you, the riches of His glorious inheritance in His holy people,
and His incomparably great power for us who believe.

EPHESIANS 1:18–19 NIV

As the ladies sat eating lunch in the mall's food court, a famous celebrity sauntered in, apparently headed to shop in one of the common stores there.

"What on earth is she doing here?" gasped one of the ladies as the others craned their necks to see the source of the growing commotion near them. Instantly, they all recognized her.

"With all her money, why would she bother coming to a place like this?" they wondered. "She could buy the whole mall!"

No matter what our socioeconomic level may be in this life, we all understand the earthly benefits wealth brings. We don't expect the people endowed with it to waste their time searching for the best bargains when they're working with unlimited resources.

And yet, as believers, we often settle for the thrift-store goods when we've really been given the keys to the kingdom.

In Christ, every spiritual blessing in the heavens belongs to us. We no longer need to scrounge through life merely hoping for some shred of peace, wisdom, purpose, or connection. We already have it all in Jesus. When we realize just how high we've been seated with Christ in the heavenly places, we begin to live here in a whole new light—like the rulers we are. We are no longer poor pawns of our enemy. We are endowed with all the wealth of heaven in order to walk in a manner worthy of our King and win the lost world back to Him.

••••••••••••••••••••••

IF THE INHERITANCE DEPENDS ON THE LAW, THEN IT NO LONGER DEPENDS ON THE PROMISE; BUT GOD IN HIS GRACE GAVE IT TO ABRAHAM THROUGH A PROMISE.

GALATIANS 3:18 NIV

CALLED OUT

You are a chosen people, a royal priesthood,
a holy nation, God's special possession,
that you may declare the praises of Him who called
you out of darkness into His wonderful light.

1 PETER 2:9 NIV

She had never seen the airport more packed, apparently everyone wanting to fly out on the same day. Her own gate was stuffed to overflowing, people crowding around the walkway entrance wanting to ensure their spot on the plane. By all appearances, it would be overbooked.

Then the attendant called out over the loudspeaker: "Attention, please. All passengers in zone one may now board the plane." She checked her ticket. *That's me!* She smiled, and people parted to make room for her as she joined the other boarding passengers.

When we're worried about whether we'll make our flight, we feel such relief at being called out of the crowd to the front of the line. Even though it's just a plane trip, it feels oddly special to be a part of the privileged group, especially when our kind of ticket is the only defining difference.

As Christians, we too have been called out of our common culture into the most privileged position as kingdom children—the defining difference between us and the world stirring from the new heart God graciously gives us. Following in our Father's footsteps, we live and love with His kingdom in focus. Like Jesus, we work to see others restored without any worry about our place in line. We rest from the pressures of pleasing other people, listening instead to God's leading alone.

In short, we live lives of distinction—but not to assert a superior position. Instead, we set ourselves apart by the way that we love others, serving with purpose every place we go.

•••••••••••••••••••••

MY PRAYER IS NOT THAT YOU TAKE THEM OUT OF THE WORLD BUT THAT YOU PROTECT THEM FROM THE EVIL ONE. THEY ARE NOT OF THE WORLD, EVEN AS I AM NOT OF IT. SANCTIFY THEM BY THE TRUTH; YOUR WORD IS TRUTH.

JOHN 17:15–17 NIV

SUPPLY SURPLUS

In the beginning God created the heavens and the earth.
Now the earth was formless and empty, darkness
was over the surface of the deep, and the Spirit
of God was hovering over the waters.
And God said, "Let there be light," and there
was light. God saw that the light was good, and
He separated the light from the darkness.

GENESIS 1:1–4 NIV

Craving something sweet, she searched her pantry. Spying a bag of chocolate chips, she smiled. *I'll bake chocolate chip cookies!* she decided. Within a matter of minutes, she had lined her counter with bowls and beaters, adding ingredients as the recipe called for each...until it came to baking soda. And eggs. *Ugghh! Why didn't I make sure I had what I needed before I started?* She groaned.

Cooking works well when we have all the right ingredients to complete the project, but it's all stress when we lack what we need. The same goes for other areas in life, as well. Maybe we see bills piling up beyond our ability to pay or loved ones struggling with needs too great for us to meet. Demands at work and friction at home further divide our attention, drain our energy, and deplete our hope for a better tomorrow. We've opened the cupboard of our souls and found it empty.

Fortunately, God's supply for godly living never runs short. For whatever we lack, we simply ask the Lord in prayer. God says that we humble ourselves and pray, He hears us. Even better, as we spend time in His presence, what we think we need begins to line up with His will. With His Spirit guiding our petition, our prayers change into beautiful trust and expectation. In the exchange we suddenly realize that our emptied reserves were no accident or oversight. They were ordained by God to drive us to Him.

IN THE PAST GOD SPOKE TO OUR ANCESTORS THROUGH THE PROPHETS AT MANY TIMES AND IN VARIOUS WAYS, BUT IN THESE LAST DAYS HE HAS SPOKEN TO US BY HIS SON, WHOM HE APPOINTED HEIR OF ALL THINGS, AND THROUGH WHOM ALSO HE MADE THE UNIVERSE.

HEBREWS 1:1–2 NIV

CHANGE OF CLOTHES

I counsel you to buy from Me gold refined in the
fire, so you can become rich; and white clothes to
wear, so you can cover your shameful nakedness;
and salve to put on your eyes, so you can see.

REVELATION 3:18 NIV

She was so excited about her first day in kindergarten that she even helped her mom pick out her outfit the night before. Arriving early, she was enamored with the colorful classroom and the other wide-eyed children she saw. It was all so wonderful—until recess. Just as soon as she pulled up on the monkey bars, swinging her legs overhead, she heard her new friends burst into laughter. In all her excitement, she had forgotten about underwear. And now her secret was exposed. In utter shame she ran to the teacher, who quickly remedied the situation with some extra clothes she had brought—just in case.

Our hearts go out when we see others experience humiliation because we know all too well how deeply shame hurts. No matter how much we try to keep our flaws covered, we worry about exposure. We don't want others to know our secret past or present struggles.

But God sees, and like the teacher on the playground, He is more than prepared to cover our shame. When we place our trust in Jesus, an incredible exchange takes place. Every failure—past, present, and future—is placed on Christ, whose death nails our guilt and shame to the cross. He covers us up with His own righteous robe, clothing us with honor that lasts forever.

When you feel the weight of shame or nagging words of condemnation coming your way, remember that Jesus already covered it all. His blood silences our accusers and fills our lives with never-ending freedom.

THOSE WHO LOOK
TO HIM ARE RADIANT;
THEIR FACES ARE NEVER
COVERED WITH SHAME.

PSALM 34:5 NIV

THE PARADISE PROGNOSIS

In all this you greatly rejoice, though now for a little while you may have had to suffer grief in all kinds of trials. These have come so that the proven genuineness of your faith—of greater worth than gold, which perishes even though refined by fire—may result in praise, glory and honor when Jesus Christ is revealed.

I PETER 1:6–7 NIV

It started out as just a tickle in her chest, causing her to cough on random occasions. After it persisted for a couple of months, she finally decided it was worth a closer look. And there it was on the scan—a preliminary explanation for her curious condition. Something was clearly growing in her lungs, but hearing the report, she felt something bigger growing in her soul: paralyzing fear. What did the future hold for her?

If she belongs to Jesus, the future holds perfect Paradise— eternity with her forever family, healthy and whole with her heavenly Father, no matter how much more time she has on this planet. Such knowledge brings perfect peace, even in scary moments like these.

While we fight for life and pray to bind Satan's schemes to steal, kill, and destroy, God's sovereign will stands supreme over all. Even in sickness and suffering, we find rest when we remember that our every breath comes from our Creator God, who not only called us into existence in the first place but fashioned our lives and the length of our days.

Remember, too, that He does not leave us to walk through life's shadows alone. Our good Shepherd stays with us through every moment. He has walked these painful places as a person Himself, and He knows how to carry us in our pain. Lean into Him, and let His love lift your worry. You and your loved ones are forever in His hands.

....

YOUR EYES SAW MY UNFORMED BODY;
ALL THE DAYS ORDAINED FOR ME
WERE WRITTEN IN YOUR BOOK
BEFORE ONE OF THEM CAME TO BE.

PSALM 139:16 NIV

BATTLE LINES

*Then the fire of the L*ORD *fell and burned up*
the sacrifice, the wood, the stones and the soil,
and also licked up the water in the trench.
When all the people saw this, they fell prostrate and cried,
*"The L*ORD*—He is God! The L*ORD*—He is God!"*

1 KINGS 18:38–39 NIV

The battle lines were drawn. Baal's 450 prophets gathered on one side; Elisha—the one prophet of God—on the other, with all of Israel watching in the background. Before it began, Elisha issued this challenge:

"How long will you waver between two opinions?"

The people considered their options, choosing not to answer Elisha. The weight of popular opinion fell to the idols. *Who would want to risk alienation?* they must have errantly thought as they stayed straddling the middle ground. Then both sides built their altars. Both cried out for help. But only one God answered, His fire consuming every part of Elisha's altar.

Today, Elisha's challenge remains. Which side will we choose? Pressure to conform to the world's way is strong, but it's God's way that always wins.

122

When we choose to stand with God, two things are sure to happen: First, we'll feel resistance and retaliation from a fallen culture that lives in darkness and despises God's ways. But in obedience, we find a real rest and a hope that is anchored in the only One who is true. We are no longer tumbled about by the restless waves of public opinion. Our eyes, hearts, and lives are fixed, strong and secure, on the One who sees us and saves our souls.

Today, tune out the jeers and sneers and take heart in God's truth instead. In time, God's glory will be known. And we are on the winning side!

TO THE ONE WHO IS VICTORIOUS,
I WILL GIVE THE RIGHT TO SIT
WITH ME ON MY THRONE,
JUST AS I WAS VICTORIOUS
AND SAT DOWN WITH
MY FATHER ON HIS THRONE.

REVELATION 3:21 NIV

WAYMAKER

Strengthen the feeble hands, steady the knees
that give way; say to those with fearful hearts,
"Be strong, do not fear; your God will come...."
Water will gush forth in the wilderness
and streams in the desert.
The burning sand will become a pool,
the thirsty ground bubbling springs.
In the haunts where jackals once lay, grass and reeds
and papyrus will grow. And a highway will be there;
it will be called the Way of Holiness;
it will be for those who walk on that Way.

ISAIAH 35:3-4, 6-8 NIV

It felt inevitable. For years, she and her husband had been at odds, the peculiar personality traits that once drew them together now driving them apart. Between work and the kids, they barely had any time together, but whenever they tried, their bitterness surfaced. As numbness set in, separation seemed the only answer, divorce and despair waiting around the corner.

They felt trapped—not unlike God's people so many years ago. The Israelites had left their homes in Egypt in hopes of finding a better life together—with God. But not long into the journey, their path ended at the Red Sea. Or so it seemed. Enemies pursued them, and certain doom awaited.

Except God had a plan all along, positioning them for a perfect miracle. As they cried out, God parted the waves. His people walked through safely, while their enemies were crushed.

Truly God has a flawless history of making a way when all hope is gone. Just look to the cross and see. Even the darkest hours give way to a new and lasting dawn in His presence. God's power raises the dead to life and opens up doors we thought were deadlocked forever.

What Red Sea roadblock are you facing today? Will you wilt in fear or turn your focus to your way-making God? Don't let your enemy convince you that all hope is lost. Every relationship and each situation in our lives serves to help us see God in a whole new light. Let your worries lead you to the God who saves, and He will light your way.

·······················

GOD IS MY STRONG FORTRESS,
AND HE MAKES MY WAY PERFECT.

II SAMUEL 22:33 NLT

HEALING HOPE

Praise the LORD, my soul,
and forget not all His benefits—
who forgives all your sins
and heals all your diseases,
who redeems your life from the pit
and crowns you with love and compassion,
who satisfies your desires with good things
so that your youth is renewed like the eagle's.

PSALM 103:2–5 NIV

When the doctor removed her bandages, the patient paused in front of the mirror. With the tumor gone, she felt so much relief. But the surgical scars looked swollen, so unsightly. She hesitated to say anything, though her expression reflected her concern. *Will I ever fully heal?* she wondered.

We often ask the Lord the same question. We've all suffered from sin's effects in this world. Though we're grateful for God's saving grace, some wounds in our soul still seem to bear scars. Though we know in our minds we are healed, when we look in the mirror we still see someone broken. *How can God ever use me when my past prevents me from appearing whole?*

Like the woman looking at her reflection, in this world we see as though peering into a darkened mirror. Often we can't make sense of the image we see and second-guess God's surgical performance.

But God sees us differently, our scars forming the seams where His light shines out the most. When we are willing to walk into our world with the message of God's grace, we no longer need to conceal our problems. Instead, we use them to point others to Christ and encourage those who hurt in the same way. Our experience and honesty may be the very key they need to unlock the door to their private pain and lead them to Jesus, who will save them, too.

•••••••••••••••••••••••

HE WAS PIERCED FOR OUR TRANSGRESSIONS,
HE WAS CRUSHED FOR OUR INIQUITIES;
THE PUNISHMENT THAT
BROUGHT US PEACE WAS ON HIM,
AND BY HIS WOUNDS WE ARE HEALED.

ISAIAH 53:5 NIV

LEADING LAMBS

He brought His people out like a flock;
He led them like sheep through the wilderness.

PSALM 78:52 NIV

When she read him the pregnancy results, her husband whooped. "I'm going to be a dad!" he shouted, and she smiled back in delight. With an embrace and a prayer of thanks, they beamed with the dreams of being perfect parents for this child and all the others God would bring into their family.

What they didn't imagine was how difficult the journey could be. As wonderful as kids are, at some point they grow—and wrestle to live with a mind of their own. Despite our best-laid plans and perfectly logical leadership, the same sweet souls we loved to cuddle when little now talk back and chart paths for their lives that we never intended. Earlier feelings of pleasure now melt into panic. *What do I do with these headstrong people?* we worry.

We look to the Lord, the same leader who led Israel out of bondage and is leading our own lives through life's long journey. Every day He delivers the power and wisdom we need to walk in His ways—but like His children, the Israelites, we must go out to seek Him. Gather the manna and ingest God's goodness daily. God promises to provide His life-giving presence when we seek Him with all our heart.

Surrender this day and your daily battles in prayer. Then rest as you hear the Shepherd's voice leading you—and your little ones—in the way you should go.

• •

IF FROM THERE YOU SEEK
THE LORD YOUR GOD, YOU WILL
FIND HIM IF YOU SEEK HIM
WITH ALL YOUR HEART AND
WITH ALL YOUR SOUL.

DEUTERONOMY 4:29 NIV

UNDER HIS FEATHERS

They did not thirst when
He led them through the deserts;
He made water flow
for them from the rock;
He split the rock
and water gushed out.

ISAIAH 48:21 NIV

Normally, feathers repel water. They have a special coating that allows birds to stay dry even in a driving rain and enables them to float on water. The same holds true for the sandgrouse, a species of bird that lives in some of earth's driest places—except for the male's breast area. Sandgrouse parents build their homes miles away from water holes to protect their babies from the predators that lurk there. But to water its own young, the father makes a sacrificial flight every day, strategizing ways to soak its special underside without detection. When the feathers have absorbed enough water, the father flies home and lets his baby chicks "milk" their water straight from his chest.

While the sandgrouse story is simply amazing, the creativity of its design shouldn't surprise us. Our God has an awesome history of quenching thirst in the driest of deserts. Wandering through the wilderness, God's people witnessed water gushing spontaneously out of boulders with just a word from their leader. Later, Jesus came to quench our spiritual thirst for good.

Are you wandering through your days with a dryness of soul? Are you worried by your own lack of devotion or enthusiasm toward what could be your life's calling? Then come to the fountain of Living Water and let your soul soak up the nourishing love of your heavenly Father. Once you are refreshed, you'll feel free to fly, bringing God's life-giving water to others as well.

· ·

WHOEVER BELIEVES IN ME,
AS SCRIPTURE HAS SAID,
RIVERS OF LIVING WATER
WILL FLOW FROM WITHIN THEM.

JOHN 7:38 NIV

NEEDING NOURISHMENT

He humbled you, causing you to hunger and then feeding
you with manna, which neither you nor your ancestors had
known, to teach you that man does not live on bread alone
but on every word that comes from the mouth of the LORD.

DEUTERONOMY 8:3 NIV

She had worked hard since the break of dawn. Loads of laundry done, dishes cleaned, she then clocked in for paid work—right on time. Daily deadlines had driven her day and she simply kept on the go until she started up the stairs to the fourth-floor copy room. Suddenly, the room started spinning. Her legs felt weak. She wondered if she was about to faint. *Am I getting sick?* she thought at first, holding herself steady by the handrail. Then she remembered. *No! I haven't eaten a thing all day!* In her busyness, she had forgotten to refuel—and her body rebelled at the neglect.

As He often does, God uses the physical world to help us visualize intangible but important spiritual truths. Just as our bodies growl with hunger when we forget to feed them, our souls grow faint with fatigue and worry when we fail to nourish them with the fuel we need most: fellowship with Jesus.

Jesus, the Bread of Life, imparts all the power and love we need for life through His Spirit, a feeding process that takes place daily. We weren't designed to work without it. The longer we go without prayer or time in God's Word, the weaker we become, until we can't walk anymore. We don't need to wonder where our passion has gone. Our souls are just spiritually depleted! But why grow faint when we have access to our Father, where we can feed on His love through prayer and praise everywhere we go?

. . . .

IN THEIR HUNGER
YOU GAVE THEM BREAD
FROM HEAVEN.

NEHEMIAH 9:15 NIV

LOOKING AT LIFE

Moses made a bronze snake and put it up on a
pole. Then when anyone was bitten by a snake
and looked at the bronze snake, they lived.

NUMBERS 21:9 NIV

She was about to get started on the dishes in the sink when she noticed the long leafy tendrils from the bush right outside her kitchen window. Bothered by the sight, she left the sponge to work her hedge clippers. But as she was cutting away, a wasp nest jostled, and its swarm of soldiers stung her hand. Now the only thing she wanted was to escape their madness and make her pain go away.

God says that our sin is a lot like those wasps—except a single sting sends us to our death. God illustrated our dire situation through the true story that happened when the Israelites wandered in the wilderness. Because of their rebellion, venomous snakes slithered into the camp and began biting—and killing—people by the thousands. But God's cure was most curious. He had Moses make a golden snake on a pole and lift it high for all to see. If the bitten people simply looked at it, they were saved.

From the very beginning, faith has played a crucial role in God's plan of salvation. Even today, the world suffers from sin's deathly venom. It's coursing through everyone's veins. But trying to be a better person on your own only ensures death. God delivers the one who looks to His Son for salvation. Trying to save ourselves is not just pointless, it's poisonous. By faith we are healed in Jesus's name!

THE STING OF DEATH IS SIN, AND THE POWER OF SIN IS THE LAW. BUT THANKS BE TO GOD! HE GIVES US THE VICTORY THROUGH OUR LORD JESUS CHRIST.

I CORINTHIANS 15:56–57 NIV

OUT OF THE TOMB

I was shown mercy so that in me, the worst of sinners,
Christ Jesus might display His immense patience
as an example for those who would believe
in Him and receive eternal life.

I TIMOTHY 1:16 NIV

As the convicted murderer stood to face his victims' families, he saw the hatred glaring from their tearstained eyes. And who could blame them? He had stolen their most precious loved ones and ruined their lives in the wake of his reckless actions. But a strange event happened in the years spent in his lonely prison cell. A chaplain met with him to share the gospel's Good News. Grateful, he received God's gift of grace. Though he knew his sins would send him to the electric chair, His Savior would pardon and receive him into Paradise. Looking out at the small crowd, he told them each how sorry he was. But who could forgive sins like that?

Our God can—and does every day. Nothing distinguishes our Father more than His amazing capacity to forgive even the most egregious sins and love people instead. To cover it all— the worst sins in the world—cost Him the life of His perfectly righteous Son. But when we surrender and receive God's free gift, sin's accusations are silenced. Murderers like Saul become world-changing Pauls in the grace-filled exchange. And the same miracle happens in our souls. Our failures fall away—as do all our self-righteous efforts. Even good works are worthless without Jesus Christ! But His blood covers it all when the broken and contrite repent from the heart and return to the Father who runs to receive us.

....

THE NINEVITES BELIEVED GOD. A FAST WAS
PROCLAIMED, AND ALL OF THEM, FROM THE
GREATEST TO THE LEAST, PUT ON SACKCLOTH....
WHEN GOD SAW WHAT THEY DID AND HOW
THEY TURNED FROM THEIR EVIL WAYS, HE
RELENTED AND DID NOT BRING ON THEM
THE DESTRUCTION HE HAD THREATENED.

JONAH 3:5, 10 NIV

THE GOD WHO SEES

She gave this name to the Lord who spoke to her:
"You are the God who sees me," for she said,
"I have now seen the One who sees me."

GENESIS 16:13 NIV

She had been kicked beyond the proverbial curb to the hot desert sands outside of town. Hagar, along with her son, Ishmael, through no fault of her own, found herself on the wrong side of Sarah's favor. They weren't needed anymore since Sarah now had her own son, Isaac, the one God promised Sarah so long ago. Without a home and weak from wandering in a hot, barren wilderness, Hagar and Ishmael lost all hope.

But God was with them. They just didn't know it.

Though every human had forsaken them, God heard their cry for help. He saw their pain and cared about their problem. Best of all, He didn't simply solve it—He opened Hagar's eyes and *showed her Him*. Even out in no-man's-land, she never walked alone. "You are the God who sees me," she cried.

And He is. So many people walk this planet hiding their private pain, alone and despairing despite the crowds around them. But we have a God who sees past our walls, deep into

138

our hearts where we hurt the most, and He cares. He sits with us in our silent sadness, encircling us in His everlasting arms, collecting every tear in His bottle because they matter. We matter to Him. Let's ask Him to open our blind eyes and believe His promises.

When we do, He lifts us from our lonely places with a new outlook on life. The one who once was lonely grows strong in God's love and follows His lead, pursuing other lost people who need to know His salvation, too.

* * * * * * * * * * * * * * * * * * * *

YOU KEEP TRACK OF ALL MY SORROWS.
YOU HAVE COLLECTED ALL MY TEARS
IN YOUR BOTTLE. YOU HAVE RECORDED
EACH ONE IN YOUR BOOK.

PSALM 56:8 NLT

DELIVERED GOODS

The weapons we fight with are not the weapons
of the world. On the contrary, they have divine power
to demolish strongholds. We demolish arguments
and every pretension that sets itself up against
the knowledge of God, and we take captive every
thought to make it obedient to Christ.

II CORINTHIANS 10:4–5 NIV

She stared hard at her boss as he walked away from her desk, having just destroyed her day. Anger stirred within the young assistant at the injustice of it all. She worked hard to keep all the plates spinning that her boss set into motion, but if anything ever went wrong (which it rarely did) she alone bore the blame. It mirrored the frustration she often felt at home, too, where complaints were plenty but affirmation was so hard to find.

What she couldn't see were the invisible, evil forces circling around her like ugly vultures, filling her mind with fear-based filth: *Your work is worthless and you are too*, they whispered. She was listening, out on the battlefield with her sword and shield on the ground.

The Bible warns us that when we choose to follow Christ, we become Satan's worst enemy. When we've been wounded by others or are weakened by overwork and isolation, we are most vulnerable to his attacks. He plays to our secret insecurities, calling God's promises into question, drawing doubt about our true identity.

Whenever we begin to feel down and defeated, we need to take notice of what we're believing. Has our enemy snuck in to steal truth and joy in some sinister thought? Through repentance and returning to what God's Word says, we render every fiery dart powerless. Following our commanding officer, Jesus, we learn to walk in warrior ways as we take every thought captive and make it obedient to Him.

SOVEREIGN LORD,
MY STRONG DELIVERER,
YOU SHIELD MY HEAD
IN THE DAY OF BATTLE.

PSALM 140:7 NIV

(FACE) PLANTING JOY

Our mouths were filled with laughter, our tongues
with songs of joy. Then it was said among the nations,
"The LORD has done great things for them."

PSALM 126:2 NIV

Everyone sat silently listening to the preacher that Sunday morning. She, however, was stressing out, secretly struggling to keep her children—two rows ahead—in line without attracting attention. She and her husband could both see them wiggling and occasionally whispering, when her husband's exasperation sent him over the top. Standing up in a huff, he stepped past each person to the main aisle, where he hoped to reach their row. Instead, he suddenly tripped over an unseen purse…and face-planted with a mighty *thud*—right in front of the preacher.

It was humbling…and it was hilarious.

And the wife was undone with belly-deep laughter, the scene so hysterical she had to fight for composure. The husband quickly rejoined her, laughing alongside her, the comic relief what they both needed most. In pursuing perfection, they had felt tremendously burdened. In laughter's release, they found renewed focus and rest in remembering God's grace and affection for imperfect people—like their kids and them—in His church.

God, after all, gave us our sense of humor! As our Maker, He sings and smiles over us as His children, loving the pure laughter that rings from our souls when we're enjoying Him and the life He has given us. Instead of worrying about how well we perform or whether other people will judge our efforts, we are freed to relax, rest, and revel in the funny faith-builders God brings along the way. The joy of the Lord is our strength!

••••••••••••••••••••

YOU SHALL GO OUT IN JOY,
AND BE LED BACK IN PEACE;
THE MOUNTAINS AND THE HILLS
BEFORE YOU SHALL BURST INTO SONG,
AND ALL THE TREES OF THE FIELD
SHALL CLAP THEIR HANDS.

ISAIAH 55:12 NRSV

FAITH FORWARD

Our children will also serve Him.
Future generations will hear about the wonders of the Lord.
His righteous acts will be told to those not yet born.
They will hear about everything He has done.
PSALM 22:30–31 NLT

He had thought he was an anomaly when he prayed to receive Christ. As far as he knew, he was the first in his whole family to make that life-changing decision. And it seemed surreal, all the steps leading up to his conversion—like some unseen hand had put all the right pieces into place.

Then the phone rang. His aunt, who lived on the other side of the country, had come across an old journal in her attic, hand-written by his great-grandfather. When it arrived in the mail and he read it, he wept. Generations before he had ever been born, his great-grandfather had been praying for him—and all the other descendants down the line, asking for their salvation. His new life in Christ was the answer to the old man's faithful, visionary prayer.

We serve a mighty God who is unbound by time constraints. When we cry out to Him for our children, grandchildren, and distant future generations, God hears and moves in times and places we may never see. Our worries about wayward generations fade as faith in God's unlimited power grows. Through prayer today, we can make an impact on people's lives all over the globe for generations to come. Let's not waste another moment, wishing times now were like they were in the past. Instead, press into God and ask Him to deliver the hope we need now and for our children's children.

* *

THE LORD WHO MADE YOU AND HELPS YOU SAYS:
DO NOT BE AFRAID, O JACOB, MY SERVANT,
O DEAR ISRAEL, MY CHOSEN ONE.
FOR I WILL POUR OUT WATER
TO QUENCH YOUR THIRST AND
TO IRRIGATE YOUR PARCHED FIELDS.
AND I WILL POUR OUT MY SPIRIT
ON YOUR DESCENDANTS, AND MY
BLESSING ON YOUR CHILDREN.

ISAIAH 44:2–3 NLT

FINISHED WORK

I am certain that God, who began
the good work within you, will continue
His work until it is finally finished
on the day when Christ Jesus returns.

PHILIPPIANS 1:6 NLT

With one hand on her hip, the other gripped her phone as she stared hard at its screen in disbelief. The man who was supposed to be helping her build her backyard deck had decided he didn't want to work on it anymore. Apparently he had been offered a more lucrative project he couldn't turn down. With half her money gone and only a half-finished deck to show for it, she sat down on the boards that would have been her steps and sighed.

When the people we rely on—even pay—to keep their promises fail us, our hope in humanity dims just a little. Why can't people just do what they say and finish whatever it was that they started in the first place? Unfortunately, people just aren't perfect. But we know the Carpenter who is! Better still, every project God begins ends in perfection every time—even when that work is us!

Jesus, the Author and Perfecter of our faith, began a good work in us the day we surrendered our lives to Him. Through the power of His unseen Spirit and His written Word, He chisels away all the waste and works in the character of Christ, building from the foundation up. Whether we one day die and go home to heaven or our Lord returns here to earth first, we can be sure of one thing: Jesus will finish what He started in each of us, presenting us to our Father without a single fault— and full of His glory.

. . . .

NOW ALL GLORY TO GOD,
WHO IS ABLE TO KEEP YOU
FROM FALLING AWAY AND WILL BRING
YOU WITH GREAT JOY INTO HIS GLORIOUS
PRESENCE WITHOUT A SINGLE FAULT.

JUDE 24 NLT

SON SHINE

Turn us again to Yourself, O God.
Make Your face shine down upon us.
Only then will we be saved.

PSALM 80:3 NLT

As the budding young artist applied more and more paint to the paper on her plastic easel, she felt proud of her picture. Though each paint container held its own color, her creativity blended them all, using one brush for trunks, treetops, and flowery fields. She wondered if anyone else in her kindergarten class was watching her wonderful masterpiece unfold. As she turned around to find an audience, she found her teacher right behind her, beaming with pleasure. The child was elated! With more energy than ever, she returned to her work.

It's amazing what we can accomplish when the people we love believe in us. Often just a simple word of encouragement or even acknowledgment of our efforts can make all the difference in whether or not we forge ahead with our ideas. It's one of the reasons the apostle Paul prayed so hard for the people who had put their faith in Christ. "God, help them see just how high and deep and wide Your love for them all actually is!" he prayed.

When we belong to Jesus, we no longer have to wonder what God thinks about us. His favor doesn't fluctuate based on how well we're drawing our picture! He's delighted that we've picked up the brush and begun applying the paint He's providing. Trust His heart, and rest with confidence in His declared love for you. This world needs to see the work of art your unique personality brings to it, treasured by God every stroke along the way.

·····················

THE LORD APPEARED TO US
IN THE PAST, SAYING:
"I HAVE LOVED YOU WITH
AN EVERLASTING LOVE;
I HAVE DRAWN YOU WITH
UNFAILING KINDNESS."

JEREMIAH 31:3 NIV

BABY FAITH

Our Lord, You will always rule,
but nations will vanish
from the earth.
You listen to the longings
of those who suffer.
You offer them hope,
and You pay attention
to their cries for help.
PSALM 10:16–17 CEV

It was the third time that morning she had to change her youngest son's diaper. Meanwhile, her two other toddlers ran like tornadoes across the room, enjoying their tired mom's distraction with other duties. Setting the baby back down to join the other two, she picked out a book she thought they'd all enjoy—at least for a few minutes. But two pages in, she was nodding off, the words jumbling together in a partial dream.

She needed more energy. Truth be told, she could use some help. But her husband was out of town and her mom six states away. So she downed another cup of coffee and tried to keep the whirlwinds contained.

But in her stupor, she missed her unseen Friend, a supernatural source of hope whose strength outperforms all the caffeine in the world! Jesus is our ever-present help in times of need, whether we are seeking to survive parenthood or to simply find a parking space so we won't be late. No need is too great or too small for our Savior's concern or capacity to solve, but He does want one small step of faith from us: instead of pulling up our bootstraps to make the best of our situation, He invites us to turn to Him for help. In the asking, we're believing that God really is involved in every detail of our day. Even diaper changes develop our faith as we find God to be a most faithful listener, helper, and friend.

• •

WE ARE CERTAIN THAT GOD WILL HEAR OUR
PRAYERS WHEN WE ASK FOR WHAT PLEASES
HIM. AND IF WE KNOW THAT GOD LISTENS
WHEN WE PRAY, WE ARE SURE THAT OUR
PRAYERS HAVE ALREADY BEEN ANSWERED.

I JOHN 5:14–15 CEV

GOD RESTORES
AND BRINGS JOY

It seemed like a dream
when the Lord brought us back
to the city of Zion.
We celebrated with laughter
and joyful songs.
In foreign nations it was said,
"The LORD has worked miracles
for His people."
And so we celebrated
because the LORD had indeed
worked miracles for us.
PSALM 126:1–3 CEV

As she watched her husband being baptized, she knew she was witnessing a miracle. Tears streamed down her face as her thoughts reflected on the long, hard road that led him here. Enduring years of his alcohol and work addiction, she had spent so much time alone, tending to their children and talking to God. When she was fearful about finances or their children's future, she leaned into the Lord even harder, looking to Him for the leadership she lacked at home, praying and believing that one day her husband would step into his God-given role.

Twenty years later, her husband's heart changed, and now he stood humbled and submitted to God's Spirit like never before. But he wasn't the only one.

In the painfully long struggle, she had experienced God's tender mercies and saving grace, day by day. Her dependence on His Spirit had grown so strong that her heart sang no matter what situation she faced. By experience, she knew her Savior was near, and she was safe.

We, too, can rest in hope regardless of our current circumstances when we realize God's goodness. He is God with us, our peace amid unpleasant realities. Today, draw closer to Him and pour out your heart's cry. Though we weep for a season, we rest knowing that with the Lord, unspeakable joy comes with the morning.

• •

THE WHOLE EARTH IS FILLED
WITH AWE AT YOUR WONDERS; WHERE
MORNING DAWNS, WHERE EVENING FADES,
YOU CALL FORTH SONGS OF JOY.

PSALM 65:8 NIV

LIVING HOPE

Jesus said to her, "I am the resurrection and the life.
The one who believes in Me will live, even though they die."

JOHN 11:25 NIV

At the funeral service, the parents were numb, their sudden shock and pain at their son's passing still unfolding. Others tried to encourage, but everyone was at a loss, wondering why God would take someone so young, so kind—such a strong Christian—home so soon. Didn't God know they needed him here more?

Whenever we lose a loved one, regardless of age, we grieve at the separation. The truth is, we weren't created to die, but humanity's sinful state seals each fate, and our souls suffer an agonizing ache in the wake of severed community. We imagine how it could have been for our loved ones and us if their lives had kept going. How can Christians cope with hope in the midst of such sadness?

Without Jesus, it would truly be the end of our story here on earth, our exit here leading to judgment and pain forever on the other side. But God, by His incredible resurrection power, has removed death's sting by opening a door to a whole new level of living hope. For the believer, passing from this life releases us from all pain and sorrow and places us immediately in Jesus's presence, where we will live for the rest of eternity. Though it grieves us to lose friends and family now, our pain is limited to our remaining time on earth. Time and friends help heal the wound, but heaven solves the problem for good. When we, too, pass into glory, all tears will be wiped away. All will be new, and God's family will reunite in one glorious wedding celebration with Jesus.

GOOD PEOPLE PASS AWAY;
THE GODLY OFTEN DIE BEFORE THEIR TIME.
BUT NO ONE SEEMS TO CARE OR WONDER WHY.
NO ONE SEEMS TO UNDERSTAND THAT GOD
IS PROTECTING THEM FROM THE EVIL TO COME.
FOR THOSE WHO FOLLOW GODLY PATHS
WILL REST IN PEACE WHEN THEY DIE.

ISAIAH 57:1–2 NLT

WORDS THAT WORK

It is the same with my word.
I send it out, and it always produces fruit.
It will accomplish all I want it to,
and it will prosper everywhere I send it.

ISAIAH 55:11 NLT

The young gardener was impatient. "Mom, it has been weeks since we planted the seeds," she explained matter-of-factly. "And look! Nothing! Nothing is coming up at all," she complained, a secret worry brewing that all their efforts were actually wasted.

"If the seed and soil are good, it will happen. We just have to wait," the mom answered. And she was right. Just a few days later, tender shoots sprang up from the barren earth, and the young girl gushed with excitement and hope.

Even as adults, we also get impatient, wanting God to cause immediate growth in us or others. In our unbelieving children or friends, we want to see signs of faith. In ourselves, we want to stop slipping into the same kinds of sin. We're seeking change and wrestling with the worry that it won't come.

But God has promised: His Word works. His truth packs so

much power that it produces fruit every single time He sends it out. When we learn what God's Word says and pray that Scripture back to Him with eager expectation for His answer, God moves. It may take days, weeks, months, or even years before we see the first sign of spring, but we will. God's Word, spoken through prayer or seasoning our conversation, releases God's Spirit to work in supernatural ways and reaps results that last into eternity.

Where do you want to see growth most? Commit it to prayer, persistently applying God's Word. Study and speak out loud the truth you learn. Then watch what God will do!

THE SON IS THE RADIANCE
OF GOD'S GLORY AND THE EXACT
REPRESENTATION OF HIS BEING,
SUSTAINING ALL THINGS
BY HIS POWERFUL WORD.

HEBREWS 1:3 NIV

THE GREAT REWARD

This is what the LORD says:
"Restrain your voice from weeping
and your eyes from tears,
for your work will be rewarded,"
declares the LORD.

JEREMIAH 31:16 NIV

Every Sunday she shows up, first for the service, and then to serve the children. Each week she plans ahead for the little Bible lesson she'll share and strategizes creative ways to make it fun and keep their attention while sowing God's Word into their fertile minds and hearts. Week in, week out, she works while few people see the effort and enthusiasm she puts into her time with the children. But there is only One whose audience she seeks, and He smiles at what He sees.

As believers, we no longer need to worry about our standing before Christ. We are made righteous through faith, and His grace won't fail us when we stand before our Father on Judgment Day. But God holds even more fun in store for those who will inherit heaven. Along with the wonder of living forever with God, we each will be rewarded according to what we did on earth.

What kind of rewards will heaven bring? God doesn't give us details, just directions to concentrate our efforts on building heavenly riches instead of earthly ones. Every smile of encouragement, every prayer for the saints, every good deed we do counts for glory because our God sees, smiles, and saves His very best rewards for heaven's grand celebration.

When we are weary of doing good day in and day out, we would do well to remember who's watching. Our good Father seeks to support us in our efforts and faithfully rewards us with the richness of His presence, both now and into eternity.

FOR THE EYES OF THE LORD RANGE
THROUGHOUT THE EARTH
TO STRENGTHEN THOSE WHOSE HEARTS
ARE FULLY COMMITTED TO HIM.

II CHRONICLES 16:9 NIV

DOWN AND UP

*God has delivered me from going
down to the pit, and I shall live
to enjoy the light of life.*

JOB 33:28 NIV

Everyone else at church seemed so happy, but she couldn't find the strength to even fake a smile. Simply getting out of bed and brushing her teeth was struggle enough. Being awake meant facing certain thoughts and feeling the pain that wouldn't go away, no matter how many prayers she prayed or praise songs she sang. She felt forever stuck in her depression and wondered why she couldn't find her way out.

These days, more light has been shed on depression's darkness than ever before. Throughout history, though, even the godliest people have grappled with it, sometimes struggling their entire lives long. As with all other illnesses we encounter in this broken world, both physical and spiritual factors have an effect. While many times prayer, praise, and Scripture study can steady our fear-filled minds, in other instances the battle trenches must be dug even deeper. God can bring amazing healing through different medicines that restore the mind's chemical balance, while time-tested therapies and counseling can work wonders alongside.

Sometimes we find supernatural healing. But God calls some people to find peace in the struggle, to seek the strength needed each moment from Him and to surround themselves with people who are standing in a stronger place and can pray for them when they can't find the words.

When you find yourself or a loved one fumbling in the darkness, don't give in to despair or dismiss the pain. Recognize the many avenues of relief, and rest in the comfort of God's never-ending care. He cradles you in the dark and has destined you for future glory.

·······················

THE LORD PROTECTS THOSE OF CHILDLIKE FAITH;
I WAS FACING DEATH, AND HE SAVED ME.
LET MY SOUL BE AT REST AGAIN, FOR THE LORD HAS
BEEN GOOD TO ME. HE HAS SAVED ME FROM DEATH,
MY EYES FROM TEARS, MY FEET FROM STUMBLING.
AND SO I WALK IN THE LORD'S PRESENCE
AS I LIVE HERE ON EARTH!

PSALM 116:6–9 NLT

PUZZLE PIECES

*It's in Christ that we find out who we are and what
we are living for. Long before we first heard of Christ
and got our hopes up, He had His eye on us, had designs
on us for glorious living, part of the overall purpose
He is working out in everything and everyone.*

EPHESIANS 1:11–12 THE MESSAGE

She always started with the edges and then moved her way
in. Her lips tight in concentration, she worked each puzzle
piece, looking for its place in the grand design. She enjoyed the
challenge, knowing that no matter how many pieces were in
the box, persistent work would pay off in the end. And it always
did, the rectangular art matching the image on the box lid.

Puzzles bring pleasure because they are solvable problems. If
we try hard enough and long enough, we can work them out.
And we often approach life the same way. As difficulties arise,
we go to great lengths to decipher the purpose behind them.
We sort out the colors and edges and work with all our might
to make sense of it all. Only sometimes we simply can't. And
we start to question whether all the right pieces were put in the
box to begin with.

Yet life with God is not flat, nor are the edges predictably straight. God's design is far more dynamic with a vibrant, living, and multidirectional dimension far beyond our limited understanding. Rest assured that if we love Him, God promises that every moment of our lives packs eternal significance, every piece with a place. Though we find joy whenever we see how some fit together, we find lasting rest when we trust that God knows what He's doing. He's shaping history—and His people in the process—for His glory and our blessing.

....

YOU INTENDED TO HARM ME,
BUT GOD INTENDED IT ALL FOR GOOD.
HE BROUGHT ME TO THIS POSITION
SO I COULD SAVE THE LIVES
OF MANY PEOPLE.

GENESIS 50:20 NLT

GAZING AND BLAZING

And we all, who with unveiled faces contemplate
the Lord's glory, are being transformed into
His image with ever-increasing glory,
which comes from the Lord, who is the Spirit.
II CORINTHIANS 3:18 NIV

Just imagine it. When Moses led the Israelites along God's winding wilderness way, he wasn't left alone to guess where to go or what to do. God Himself met with Moses, often more than a month at a time, imparting His heart so Moses, the mediator, could teach God's people. And something visibly miraculous resulted from the intimate exchange: Moses's face glowed with God's glory. It was such an unsettling sight when he returned to camp that the Israelites asked him to cover it with a cloth. To them, a glowing human was just too...supernatural.

Now picture this: God still brings His glory into earthly temples in the same dramatic way! Even though our bodies may be aging or our appearance may be "nothing to see," something supernatural happens when we sit at God's feet and soak in His glory. As we allow our thoughts to dwell on His goodness, power, provision, and love, our lives begin to glow with inexplicable peace and purpose. The dark world around us may wonder or wince at its brightness, but we don't need to cover God's brilliance. As the little child's song says, we change the world when we let God's light shine.

Today, let us make time to marvel at God's majesty, drawing close to Him in silent reverence as we listen for what He has to say and how He reveals His heart. As we do, His Spirit inside us renews our strength, fills us with hope, and sets our whole life ablaze with His passion and glory.

WE DO NOT LOSE HEART. THOUGH OUTWARDLY
WE ARE WASTING AWAY, YET INWARDLY
WE ARE BEING RENEWED DAY BY DAY.

II CORINTHIANS 4:16 NIV

THE WAY OUT

*So then, since we have a great High Priest who
has entered heaven, Jesus the Son of God, let us
hold firmly to what we believe. This High Priest
of ours understands our weaknesses, for He faced
all of the same testings we do, yet He did not sin.
So let us come boldly to the throne of our gracious
God. There we will receive His mercy, and we
will find grace to help us when we need it most.*

HEBREWS 4:14–16 NLT

The audience watched in fearful anticipation. What the magician attempted to do seemed doomed to disaster. Shackled by thick chains around his feet and his hands tied behind his back, he was supposed to escape the small, clear box where he stood—even as it was filling with water. Soon it was over his head, and everyone held their breath while they waited to see what would happen.

Watching escape tricks can be fun and entertaining, but wrestling with real-life temptations and traps feels more traumatic. We wonder if we have the will or wits to make it out of the situation alive.

But God is the One waiting for us to wake up and realize He's handed us the key that unlocks our chains. No matter what difficulty or daunting temptation we face, we walk away free when we go to God for help in the middle of it. Jesus Himself understands our issues because He experienced life on this earth just like we do—only He did it without sin. When we feel doomed to repeat our same sinful behavior, we have a way out. It's Jesus Himself, who comes to our aid when we call out to Him as the water is rising.

Where or when do you feel destined to failure? Is it when you walk to the fridge? When you turn on the computer? When you enter into conversation with those people? Recognize the rut for what it is and run to the One who will show you the way out.

• •

NO TEMPTATION HAS OVERTAKEN YOU EXCEPT WHAT IS COMMON TO MANKIND. AND GOD IS FAITHFUL; HE WILL NOT LET YOU BE TEMPTED BEYOND WHAT YOU CAN BEAR. BUT WHEN YOU ARE TEMPTED, HE WILL ALSO PROVIDE A WAY OUT SO THAT YOU CAN ENDURE IT.

I CORINTHIANS 10:13 NIV

GOD'S NATURE

Look to the LORD and His strength;
seek His face always.
I CHRONICLES 16:11 NIV

It was his little girl's favorite game. Every time they went on family walks through the woods, the dad would issue his challenge: a nickel for every neat nature surprise she could find, but a whole quarter for the coolest discoveries (think lizards, frogs, snakes—anything living). She loved it! Every walk became an amazing adventure, her senses fine-tuned and focused on every unusual motion, color, or sound that could potentially score more reward. In the end, she cashed in her points at the ice cream shop, where she and her dad remembered together all the wonderful scenes they had experienced.

But God doesn't want the adventure game to end as we grow up. As our loving Father, He continues to lead each one of us daily on the wildest journey of our lives. When we learn to pay attention to how God is working all around us, a whole new world of wonder and awe unfolds before our eyes. Suddenly our conversation with the cashier becomes a life-changing encounter. The wildflower springing up from the cracked sidewalk is a sign—that God's loving nature is seen everywhere we go. As we keep our eyes peeled for God's purpose—even in the mundane moments—we find a million beautiful miracles right around us. Joy and peace and purpose are ours every step of the way as we watch with anticipation to see God's goodness in all its glorious forms and then celebrate what we see in sweet praise to Him.

....

THEY CELEBRATE YOUR
ABUNDANT GOODNESS AND JOYFULLY
SING OF YOUR RIGHTEOUSNESS.

PSALM 145:7 NIV

HOLDING OUT

The LORD God is our sun and our shield.
He gives us grace and glory.
The LORD will withhold no good thing
from those who do what is right.

PSALM 84:11 NLT

As he offered excuses, she stared at him, completely stunned by this turn of events. He was the perfect Christian guy, and she had given so much of her time and effort to the relationship. She had prayed for God's direction and felt so much peace pursuing this path. It just seemed perfect. Except now it wasn't, because he was backing out. Anger invaded her thoughts, followed by bitterness—aimed first at her ex-boyfriend but later at God. She felt tricked, mistreated. *If God loved me, why would He let this happen?* she let her mind wonder.

We all have to watch our hearts and minds when life doesn't work out the way we planned. Our enemy is ready and eager to sow seeds of discontent and distrust as we question what God is doing. Like Eve in the Garden when the serpent second-guessed God's goodness, we're tempted to believe that God is holding out on us.

But God invites us to walk away from that temptation into a place of utter trust. When we can't figure out why God has blocked our path, we can lean even harder on His leading; let go of our demanding; allow the Spirit to change our thinking while healing our wounded hearts. When we keep our hands open to God, we experience deeper rest. In the resting, we realize God's plan—always drawing us closer to His presence—was far better than what we imagined in the first place.

SO IF YOU SINFUL PEOPLE KNOW
HOW TO GIVE GOOD GIFTS
TO YOUR CHILDREN, HOW MUCH MORE
WILL YOUR HEAVENLY FATHER GIVE
GOOD GIFTS TO THOSE WHO ASK HIM.

MATTHEW 7:11 NLT

REST RESTORED

The Spirit of the Sovereign LORD is on me, because the LORD
has anointed me to proclaim good news to the poor. He has
sent me to bind up the brokenhearted, to proclaim freedom
for the captives and release from darkness for the prisoners...
to bestow on them a crown of beauty instead of ashes, the oil
of joy instead of mourning, and a garment of praise instead of
a spirit of despair. They will be called oaks of righteousness,
a planting of the LORD for the display of His splendor.
ISAIAH 61:1, 3 NIV

Her daughter had a wonderful idea to plant a garden. So the two took a trip to the local nursery, picked out pots and seeds, shovels and fertilizer, then formed a plan about who would do what as they weeded, prepped, and planted their garden. They worked at it for hours in the hot spring sun, digging holes and putting in seeds until darkness took over.

But in the morning, they both woke up to disappointment. Apparently intrigued by all the activity, their dog had dug up all they had planted. The yard was a ruined mess, the destruction seemingly beyond repair.

Sometimes we experience life like that garden. We put in the hard work of parenting or preparing for a long-held dream, only to wake up years down the road feeling like either we or someone else has ruined our plans, utterly destroying our hope.

But in Jesus, hope always grows. Though our garden may no longer spring up in the pattern we planned, God's Word promises to bear fruit—even in the unlikeliest places—when we stay surrendered to Him. Wayward children often return home and dreams rerouted by devastating roadblocks wind up working out after all under God's sovereign plan.

When reflections on the past bring regret, remember that God restores ALL things. Nothing remains broken in His hands. He is the master Gardener who tills our souls' soil and sends the rain for our nourishment, though we'd rather it stay sunny all the time. Waiting and trusting in His way, we'll witness the growth of a richer faith—with roots winding deeper into His love.

•••••••••••••••••••••••

I WILL RESTORE TO YOU THE YEARS THAT THE SWARMING LOCUST HAS EATEN, THE HOPPER, THE DESTROYER, AND THE CUTTER, MY GREAT ARMY, WHICH I SENT AMONG YOU. YOU SHALL EAT IN PLENTY AND BE SATISFIED, AND PRAISE THE NAME OF THE LORD YOUR GOD, WHO HAS DEALT WONDROUSLY WITH YOU. AND MY PEOPLE SHALL NEVER AGAIN BE PUT TO SHAME.

JOEL 2:25–26 ESV

CARRIED

*The horse is made ready
for the day of battle,
but victory rests with the LORD.*

PROVERBS 21:31 NIV

When she awoke, she didn't need to check her calendar. She knew what day it was. For over a month she had been prepping her home and scouring every place to find empty moving boxes. Yesterday they were finally all filled with her family's belongings. Now she just needed the movers to arrive. Without their help, she'd be up a creek—without any of her stuff. She was a smart and strong woman, but she knew her limitations. When the load was too much for her, she let someone stronger take over and handle the rest.

It's a great strategy, the very kind our Savior says works in His kingdom, when we strike the right balance. Whenever God calls us to move from where we are, we may feel uncertain at first. How can we know God's will, and what's the best way to get there? Certainly anxieties often lessen with a semblance of order, so putting a good plan in place may be the perfect solution for some of the stress!

But the secret to real rest lies in relying on who's strongest. While God has given us physical bodies to think and brainstorm, plan and plot, He alone has the understanding and strength we need for life to work. More than that, He infuses our earthly efforts with supernatural power, wielding impact beyond this life into eternity.

Today, don't wear yourself out, trying to wing it on your own. Let your Father do the heavy lifting as you lay your needs before Him in prayer.

....

IT DOES NOT, THEREFORE,
DEPEND ON HUMAN DESIRE
OR EFFORT, BUT ON GOD'S MERCY.

ROMANS 9:16 NIV

ANCIENT WAYS

This is what the LORD says:
"Stand at the crossroads and look;
ask for the ancient paths,
ask where the good way is,
and walk in it, and
you will find rest for your souls."

JEREMIAH 6:16 NIV

Her granddaughter looked up at her in earnest, eyes twinkling with eagerness.

"I don't know, honey," the grandmother answered, uncertain, eyeing the bike she was supposed to get on and ride. "I haven't done that in many years." But love for her granddaughter compelled her, so she gathered her wits and all the energy she had and hopped on the bike.

As they rode down the sidewalk, wind in their hair, the woman's mind flooded with memories. She remembered what it felt like to be adventurous and fun, free from the worries the adult world brought with it. Her feet pedaled faster and her hands steered with skill just as they did when she was younger, the rhythm and joy of childhood returning to her heart.

Some things in life just feel right. They settle in our souls like *This is how it should be.*

We need to listen. The One who whispers behind us which way we should go in life sounds louder when we return to the simplicity of childlike faith. And Jesus says, *Come. Return to the place where you once knew grace and love and forgiveness.* The fountain of joy and peace still flows there, the Lord of all eager for you to experience Him again like when your faith first began.

Life in this world can slowly lead our hearts astray until our souls feel hard and dry. When we wonder what went wrong, God says to return to the ancient paths. Place your trust again in the only One who's proven true, and you will find your way.

●●●●●●●●●●●●●●●●●●●●●

START CHILDREN OFF
ON THE WAY THEY SHOULD GO,
AND EVEN WHEN THEY ARE OLD
THEY WILL NOT TURN FROM IT.

PROVERBS 22:6 NIV

FIRE POWER

Fear of the LORD leads to life,
bringing security and protection from harm.
PROVERBS 19:23 NLT

The young boy watched his father tend the fire. Flames billowed and sparks shot up into the night sky whenever he carefully moved the logs to allow more oxygen to fuel it. It was beautifully warm, mesmerizing...magical. So when the father went around their tent to gather more wood, the boy eased closer to play with the glowing embers. But in stirring them, the heat surged up and sparks flew out, singeing his face and hands. Suddenly he knew a new level of respect for fire's power.

God, the Creator of fire, uses the common energy to help us understand Him better, too. His call to come and circle around His presence warms our hearts and souls, and we grow comfortable with who we think He is.

But He is far greater.

Though His love, forgiveness, and mercy are certain, God is supernatural. Our finite minds can't contain all who He is, His power and wisdom so far stronger and higher than our own. We warm ourselves in His love and draw comfort from His grace, but our knees drop down in reverence when we reflect on who He really is.

What an awesome privilege we have to walk with our Maker! The Great I AM who blazed before Moses on God's holy mountain beckons us to come closer this day. Let us draw near to our Father in full assurance of His love. And let us live in reverence, following His ways, as our fear of the Lord leads us to true worship and wisdom.

• •

I LISTEN CAREFULLY
TO WHAT GOD THE LORD IS SAYING,
FOR HE SPEAKS PEACE
TO HIS FAITHFUL PEOPLE.
BUT LET THEM NOT RETURN
TO THEIR FOOLISH WAYS.
SURELY HIS SALVATION IS NEAR
TO THOSE WHO FEAR HIM,
SO OUR LAND WILL BE FILLED
WITH HIS GLORY.

PSALM 85:8–9 NLT

PRAY FOR WISDOM

If you need wisdom, ask our generous God,
and He will give it to you.
He will not rebuke you for asking.

JAMES 1:5 NLT

The storm raged all around the passenger plane, despite the pilot's efforts to avoid it. Lightning bolts split the sky outside as the passengers tightly gripped their seats, many sending up prayers for protection. Dark and menacing clouds veiled outside vision, so the pilot radioed the tower for assistance. The ground's radar capabilities could track his course in a reliable way and reroute him to a better path. As he listened for directions, he dodged the worst parts of the storm and eventually landed the plane in safety.

In life, we often feel like the pilot of that plane. We're supposed to be in charge of our families, our careers, even planning for the future, but we can't see past the windshield, which is a problem no matter what kind of weather is outside.

But we always have a strong tower to call on who helps us find our way. None of us here on this planet have the perspective we need to navigate life well on our own—we were designed to radio for help! God's Spirit and His Word are true, both working in tandem to impart the wisdom we lack.

Whenever you find yourself fearing the unknown and trying to find your way through dark places, run to the tower for wisdom and guidance. God promises to give you all that you need as He gently steers you toward deeper trust in Him.

• •

THE NAME OF THE LORD
IS A STRONG TOWER;
THE RIGHTEOUS MAN RUNS
INTO IT AND IS SAFE.

PROVERBS 18:10 ESV

HOPE SINGS

Why am I discouraged?
Why is my heart so sad? I will put my hope in God!
I will praise Him again—my Savior and my God!
Now I am deeply discouraged, but I will remember you—
even from distant Mount Hermon, the source of the Jordan,
from the land of Mount Mizar. I hear the tumult of the
raging seas as your waves and surging tides sweep over me.
But each day the LORD *pours His unfailing love upon me,*
and through each night I sing His songs,
praying to God who gives me life.

PSALM 42:5–8 NLT

As she swept the floor (for the umpteenth time this week), her mind wandered with a wide range of thoughts. Sometimes she felt angry at all the junk left on counters and floors, her family failing to notice the toll their negligence took on her and her work. But just then she saw an old toy tucked into a corner, and warmer sentiments filled her.

Like a seesaw in her mind, her emotions rose and fell depending on her focus, both positive and negative fighting for the high seat. The fight in her head sapped more strength than the sweeping! Even in solitude, she needed some peace! So she turned on some praise music. And that move made all the difference.

We may not understand why music moves us in ways nothing else can, but we know by experience that it does. But music that lifts up our Lord's name in praise does even more, taking our thoughts to a whole new level and transforming our minds to make them like His. As we listen to truth and agree in song, our souls are soothed in God's all-encompassing goodness. Petty grievances and task-driven agendas give way to repentance, and declaring God's greatness brings light to our darkness. In His presence, our minds change and our souls are moved to work in sync with the Spirit. Praise is God's secret weapon that silences distraction and focuses are hearts where they belong— at home with our Lord.

* * * * * * * * * * * * * * * * * * * *

PRAISE THE LORD! HOW GOOD
TO SING PRAISES TO OUR GOD!
HOW DELIGHTFUL AND HOW FITTING!

PSALM 147:1 NLT

BELIEVING BETTER

*"You will not succeed by your own strength or by
your own power. The power will come from my
Spirit," says the Lord of heaven's armies.*

ZECHARIAH 4:6 ICB

The longer she sat in her class, the more her stomach turned and twisted. *How am I ever going to get this done?* she worried as she scanned her calendar, calculating all the assignments she'd been given for the week. The mounting pressure surged like a rising tsunami. She felt certain she would drown. *How are humans supposed to survive so much stress?* she silently wondered.

By nature, we worry when pressures rise. It seems like our hearts can't help but buckle under the heavy loads we bear, and we labor hard to either tackle and tame every towering challenge or take a leave of absence from any effort at all.

But Jesus invites us to a better way—one that requires work, but lighter than the kind we've grown accustomed to do. He says, "Believe."

When we fear that we're going to fail, we can believe that He's with us and will keep us from stumbling. When we question our future, we keep our eyes on Him because He's already there. And when we're tired from faith's fight, His name is our refuge. We find peace in God's unfailing promises—when we fully believe He's as good as His Word.

And what if we find ourselves failing in belief? By faith, move forward in obedience anyway. As we follow Christ's directions to come to Him for relief, we find our belief grows stronger—and our Savior was right, after all. His yoke is easy and His burden is light. In our unbelief, we can ask for more faith. No matter what our feelings, our Father remains faithful.

••••••••••••••••••••••

NOW WE WHO HAVE BELIEVED ENTER THAT REST, JUST AS GOD HAS SAID, "SO I DECLARED ON OATH IN MY ANGER, 'THEY SHALL NEVER ENTER MY REST.'" AND YET HIS WORKS HAVE BEEN FINISHED SINCE THE CREATION OF THE WORLD.

HEBREWS 4:3 NIV

STEADY STRENGTH

Therefore everyone who hears these words
of Mine and puts them into practice is like
a wise man who built his house on the rock.

MATTHEW 7:24 NIV

It took everything within you just to get inside the gym. Now you're sitting on the bench press, wondering if it also works for short naps. *I don't think I can do this,* you mumble under your breath, hating the heaviness of the weights now in your hands. Spurred on by the sleek physiques that seem to encircle you, you press on, repeating the count until the set is complete. *Excruciating,* you conclude. But tomorrow, you know you'll try again. Getting back in shape is simply hard work. But every day, your courage and conviction for a healthier you grows, and you can feel yourself growing stronger.

The same is true for the spirit inside us. Even if we feel instinctively weak spiritually, by God's grace we will grow stronger with each act of obedience. Instead of heavy lifting, we daily lay our weights down through prayer, developing a greater dependence on God's guidance and resources. As we press through passages in God's Word, His Spirit works understanding and reverence into our soul. And as we remember and reflect on what God says, our ability and desire to do life God's way grows each day.

Scripture warns us that trials will come our way, but if we've trained our minds to stick to God's truth, we'll stand through the storms. Obstacles become only opportunities for God to display His amazing faithfulness. As we press on, others will see our strength and seek to know the God who empowers us to stay so steady.

· · · · · · · · · · · · · · · · · · · ·

SURELY MY ARM WILL STRENGTHEN HIM.
THE ENEMY WILL NOT GET THE BETTER OF HIM;
THE WICKED WILL NOT OPPRESS HIM.

PSALM 89:21–22 NIV

THE PERFECT PLACE

Let the peace of Christ rule in your hearts, since as members
of one body you were called to peace. And be thankful.
COLOSSIANS 3:15 NIV

It was late afternoon, and she had a little time on her hands before beginning dinner. Sitting down at her computer, she started to surf. Pop-up messages reminded her of people she hadn't seen in years, and before she knew it, she was scrolling through photo after perfect photo, looking at all the fun and fellowship everyone else seemed to be having. Even as she clicked "Like," she couldn't help wanting…wishing…wondering if her life (with all her worries) would ever be that good.

Then she went outside. The sun was setting behind the trees, brilliant streaks of pink and gold gilding a faint blue sky. A light breeze blew as the summer cicadas stirred in evening celebration. She sank onto her patio chair to enjoy the show, God's glory cast through chorus and color. In her pleasure, she felt God's presence. In His nearness, she gave thanks, her gratitude for all God's goodness washing away the discontent.

In giving thanks, we find our rightful place in this world and rest for our searching souls. We are the recipients of God's extraordinary grace, the object of His undeserved favor. In all the moments of our lives—the fun and the fearful, the successes and the failures—we live loved. All of eternity, beginning even before our birth, has been purchased for us at the highest price, our future secured by our loving Savior. The beauty of creation sings with worship and wonder at such extravagant love, lavished on us, God's beloved children. Let us join in with the song!

REJOICE IN THE LORD ALWAYS. I WILL SAY IT AGAIN: REJOICE! LET YOUR GENTLENESS BE EVIDENT TO ALL. THE LORD IS NEAR. DO NOT BE ANXIOUS ABOUT ANYTHING, BUT IN EVERY SITUATION, BY PRAYER AND PETITION, WITH THANKSGIVING, PRESENT YOUR REQUESTS TO GOD. AND THE PEACE OF GOD, WHICH TRANSCENDS ALL UNDERSTANDING, WILL GUARD YOUR HEARTS AND YOUR MINDS IN CHRIST JESUS.

PHILIPPIANS 4:4–7 NIV

Just think,
you're here not by chance
but by God's choosing.
His hand formed you
and made you
the person you are.
He compares you to no one else—
you are one of a kind.
You lack nothing
that His grace can't give you.
He has allowed you to be here
at this time in history
to fulfill His special purpose
for this generation.
ROY LESSIN

DaySpring

Dear Friend,

This book was prayerfully crafted with you, the reader, in mind—every word, every sentence, every page—was thoughtfully written, designed, and packaged to encourage you...right where you are this very moment. At DaySpring, our vision is to see every person experience the life-changing message of God's love. So, as we worked through rough drafts, design changes, edits, and details, we prayed for you to deeply experience His unfailing love, indescribable peace, and pure joy. It is our sincere hope that through these Truth-filled pages your heart will be blessed, knowing that God cares about you—your desires and disappointments, your challenges and dreams.

He knows. He cares. He loves you unconditionally.

BLESSINGS!
THE DAYSPRING BOOK TEAM
